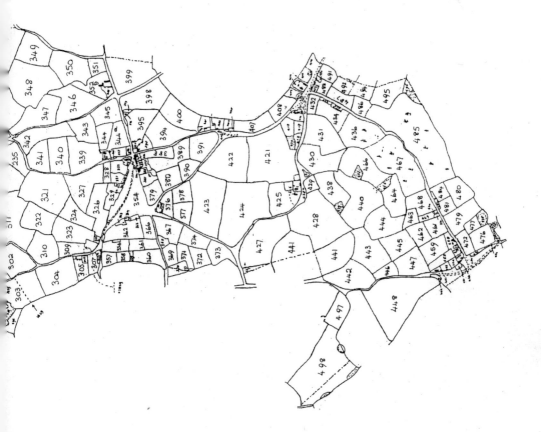

Datchworth parish in 1839,
based on the tithe map (HALS: DSA4/34/2)

An Account of my Receipts of Tythes upon
the Harvest 1715 —   1716

	Wid Whittenborough	00 : 10 : 00
	Jaine Crawley in part	04 : 00 : 00
Sep.r	Wil.m Pennyfather in part	02 : 03 : 00
	of John Blindall in full	00 : 13 : 00
Nov.r 19	Received of Wil.m Hatton in full	01 : 00 : 00
19	Received of Wm Butterfield for 15 Acres of Gilt Crop and	00 : 05 : 00
	20 Acres of Edge Crop and five Tithings for small Tythes	00 : 12 : 00
19	Received of Wil.m Pendred in full	05 : 09 : 00
19	Received of Wil.m Kimpton 4 Acres of Gilt 32 of Edge	03 : 00 : 00
19	Received of John Whitfield 9 Acres of Edge 3 of Gilt	00 : 10 : 00
19	Received of John Bassett jun.r in full	01 : 00 : 00
19	Received of Jane Crawley in full	00 : 01 : 08
20	Received of John Bassett sen.r	00 : 10 : 00
20	Received of Rowland Mardell for Turnips in y.e years 1715	00 : 12 : 00
	Received of him for other small Tythes	00 : 17 : 00
	Received of him for Tythe Turnips in the year 1716	00 : 12 : 00
	Received of him for other small Tythes 10 nichs 1716	
	Received of him for his Uncle and Aunt Grimsall in the	04 : 00 : 00
1716	Chancek	
Feb.y 1.th	Received of Ed: Mardell of Wolmore Green for 3 Acres of Pigeon	00 : 06 : 00
	Received of Tho.s Poole in full the sum of 20li	20 : 00 : 00
	Received of Wil.m Wally in full	08 : 10 : 00
	Received of Tho.s Bellin in full	01 : 04 : 00
	Received of Tho.s Colvin in full	00 : 10 : 00
	Received of John Midard in full	00 : 10 : 00
	Received of Ed: Mardell 3 Acres of Edge	00 : 06 : 00
	Received of James Blindall 2 Acres of Gilt & 10 of Edge	00 : 10 : 00
	Received of John Barr in full	00 : 15 : 00
	Received of mr Hudson	00 : 10 : 00
	Received of Tho.s Freeman	01 : 01 : 00
	Received of Tho.s Venables	00 : 04 : 00
	Received of mr Miles for small Tythes	01 : 10 : 00
	Received of him for Turnips upon the Glebe	03 : 00 : 00
Feb.y 14	Received of Wil.m Pennyfather in full for Lords Hill	01 : 17 : 00
	Received of Joseph Mansel	00 : 05 : 00
	Rec.d of Edward Pennyfather	00 : 07 : 00
	Received of Benjamin Uncle in part	00 : 05 : 00
	Received of Jon Venables	00 : 04 : 00
Sep.r 30 1718	Received of Widow Mardell in part for 6 years	00 : 05 : 00
	Received of Jon Smith of Bull Green	00 : 01 : 06
Oct.r 18	Received of Tho.s Hanny	03 : 05 : 00
		80 : 14 : 02

Contents

Illustrations

Acknowledgements

Preparation for this volume has relied heavily on access to documents at Hertfordshire Archives and Local Studies, an immensely pleasurable activity thanks to Susan Flood and her cheerful and enthusiastic team of archivists and assistants. In particular, Susan's observations and advice relating to the assembly of the component parts of the volume have been very helpful. I am also indebted to specialists in their fields, in particular, Phillip Judge who has prepared maps so efficiently and Anita Pond for creating the fine dust jacket; also, to friends who have been badgered for help, particularly Toddy Hamilton-Gould and John Wallace for advice on matters equine and agricultural respectively and John Vaughan-Shaw for his help in Latin translation. Professor Peter Marshall and Dr Evelyn Lord kindly read the text and made some valuable contributions and comments, all gratefully received. Special thanks go to Dr Heather Falvey whose encouragement enabled this volume to be started and whose guidance and patience have been invaluable in its completion.

General editorial method

- Pages in the original document are not numbered. The editor has assigned page numbers in bold type in square brackets thus: **[1]**
- The order of the pages has been left as found except for **[1]** and **[8]**. **[1]** has been placed last and **[8]** is after **[4]**.
- Original spellings have been retained with capital letters where they occur. Some punctuation has been inserted to improve clarity of meaning. Surnames and place-names have been left as they were written in the text and Christian names have been silently extended where appropriate. All names have been standardized in the footnotes
- Standard early modern abbreviations such as w^{ch} (which) have been silently extended, and others such as Q^r (Quarter) have been treated similarly. B^l has been extended in square brackets thus: B[ushe]l to distinguish this spelling from Hawtayne's version: Bushill. Other unusual abbreviations have been extended in square brackets
- Words in slanted brackets \thus/ were inserted by the original author
- Words crossed through ~~thus~~ were deleted by the original writer
- Illegible deletions have been rendered thus : *illeg*
- Barely legible text is preceded by a question mark and enclosed in square brackets eg [?28]
- A question mark after a word in square brackets signifies its possible meaning eg [full?]
- Editorial notes are given in italic text in square brackets eg [*Total*]
- (Round brackets) used in the original text have been reproduced
- Headings in **Bold normal text** appear in the original, those in ***Bold italic text*** have been added by the editor
- Latin words have been written in italics eg *vide contra*
- Underlining has been included where it occurs in the original
- Money: 12 pennies (12d) = 1 shilling (1s); 20 shillings =1 pound (£1)
- Capacity for dry goods eg grain: 4 pecks = 1 bushel; 8 bushels = 1 quarter; 5 bushels = 1 load (in Hertfordshire)
- Area: 1 acre = 4 roods, 1 rood = 40 poles, 1 pole = 30¼ square yards

Abbreviations used in the text and footnotes

AHH	Archdeaconry of Huntingdon, Hitchin Division
ASA	Archdeaconry of St Albans
BLARS	Bedfordshire and Luton Archives and Record Service
CCED	Clergy of the Church of England Database, www.theclergydatabase.org.uk
HALS	Hertfordshire Archives and Local Studies
HRS	Hertfordshire Record Society
IGI	International Genealogical Index, www.familysearch
OED	*Oxford English Dictionary*
VCH	*Victoria County History*

Dates

As the old-style calendar was in use, the modernized year has been shown from 1 January to 24 March; thus, for the date 3 March 1714, the year is written 1714/15. On two occasions (**[7]** and **[16]**), the rector himself used this style of dating, writing consecutive years as a sort of fraction. If the year was omitted in the original, the suggested year has been added in square brackets, for example, [1711]. If the year is included in the heading, it has not been repeated at the top of the left hand column. All dates in the left hand column have been standardized in the following way: 1719 May 8.

References to towns and villages

Unless otherwise stated all towns and villages mentioned are in Hertfordshire.

Introduction

December 1680 was notable nationally for the appearance of a spectacular comet and locally in Farthinghoe (Northamptonshire) for the birth of William Hawtayne, son of Catherine and William Hawtayne. The first prime minister, Robert Walpole, was appointed during Hawtayne's lifetime, in which there were many changes in the monarchy; indeed Hawtayne himself rubbed shoulders with royalty. Behind the tithing book of Datchworth that is reproduced in this volume, there is hidden a family man who not only had a reputation as a respected preacher but also managed to maintain diverse professional responsibilities. The annual tithe collection may well have been a chore as this extract from a contemporary poem suggests.

> This priest, he merry is and blithe
> Three quarters of a year;
> But oh! it cuts him like a scythe,
> When tithing time draws near.
>
> The dinner comes, and down they sit:
> Were e'er such hungry folk?
> There's little talking and no wit;
> It is no time to joke.
>
> At length the busy time begins.
> 'Come, neighbours, we must wag'[1]
> The money chinks, down drop their chins,
> Each lugging out his bag.
>
> One talks of mildew and of frost,
> And one of storms of hail,
> And one of pigs that he has lost
> By maggots at the tail.

The Revd William Unwin of Stock (Essex) was the inspiration for this poem written by William Cowper (1731-1800), a Hertfordshire man born in Berkhamsted.[2]

---

[1] 'wag', in this context, meant to depart or to be off (*OED*)
[2] Verses from *The Yearly Distress,* by William Cowper, (*The Poetical Works of William Cowper with a memoir by Charles Whitehead* (1849), pp156, 157)

INTRODUCTION

Datchworth

Datchworth is situated somewhat higher than most of the surrounding parishes and the church is in a commanding position visible from far around. One early eighteenth century map of Hertfordshire (see rear end paper) shows Datchworth (in Broadwater Hundred) in relation to the market town of Hertford, roughly seven miles to the south-east where Hawtayne sold his goods and occasionally bought farming equipment.[3] Other places significant in Hawtayne's career were Shephall, just north of Datchworth and Elstree (also called Idelstrey), some 19 miles south of Datchworth, to the west of Totteridge.

The parish is typical of a dispersed settlement consisting of several 'Greens', such as Burnham Green, Bulls Green, Govers Green and, of course, Datchworth Green, some of which are mentioned in Hawtayne's book. Although today Datchworth Green represents the hub of village activity, the true centre of the village is at the church, as it was in Hawtayne's day. In Domesday Book land in Datchworth was described as being roughly five hides and by then most of it belonged to Westminster Abbey.[4] This was land that had been given to the Abbey by King Edgar (959 to 975). The principal manor was that of Datchworth and it was the lord of this manor that held the advowson of the church from an unknown date. Evidence of an agreement in 1192 between the Abbot of Westminster and Hugh de Bocland, lord of the manor at the time, that he should pay 20 shillings to the Abbot, suggests that the church probably dates from the twelfth century, of which the nave is the only remaining part. A second manor, Hawkin's Hall, was partially in the parish of Datchworth but also spread into the neighbouring parish of Watton-at-Stone.[5]

At the date of the publication of *The Victoria County History* (1908) the parish was said to have an area of just over 2000 acres and roughly three-quarters of the land was arable. The rest was either grass or woodland. Thus described, the rural nature of the parish is clear and the agricultural environment that existed then would have been similar 200 years earlier, in Hawtayne's time, but functioned, no doubt, at a slower pace.

---

[3] Sir Henry Chauncy, *The Historical Antiquities of Hertfordshire,* (First published 1700, reproduced Dorking 1975).
[4] One hide represented an area sufficient to support a family for a year. (K Tiller, *English local history an introduction,* (Gloucestershire, 2002) pp28-30)
[5] W Page (ed), *VCH, a History of Hertfordshire,* (1908), vol III, pp78-81

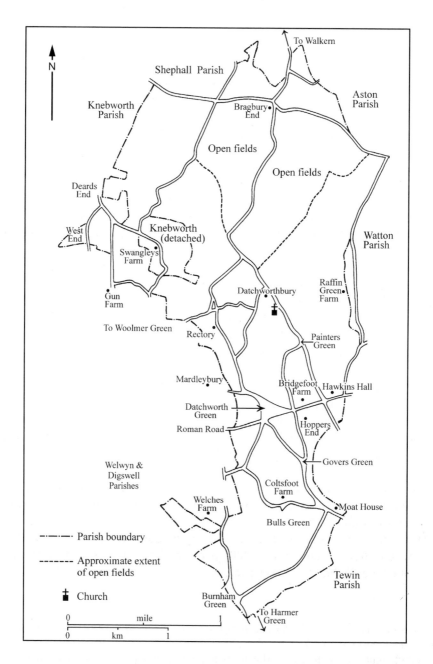

Figure 1 Datchworth Parish
The outline has been taken from the 1839 tithe map (HALS: DSA4/34/2)

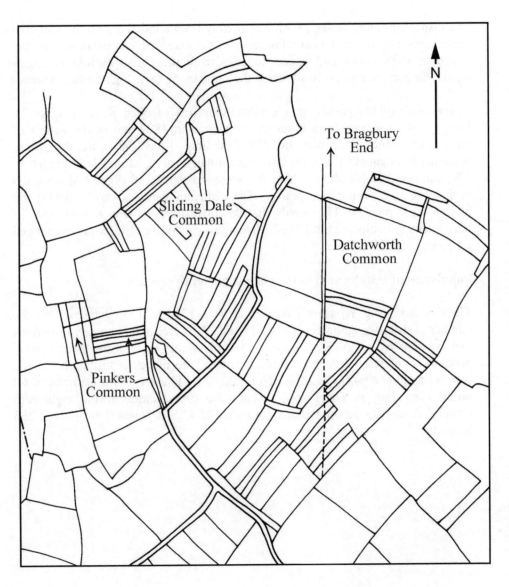

Figure 2
Remains of open fields in Datchworth in 1829 (HALS: DP/33/29/2)

INTRODUCTION

The dispersed nature of the parish has already been alluded to and the scattered settlements may be seen when viewing the tithe map that accompanied the tithe award in 1838 (front end paper) together with the parish outline Figure 1. Again, the picture was probably much the same in the early eighteenth century.

In the north of the parish, was a substantial area of open fields, (Figure 1). Figure 2 is an extract from a survey completed in 1829 and shows details of these fields as they were then. In 1839 at the time of the tithe award, the picture is similar but many of the strips have been amalgamated, as visible in Figure 3.[6] The numbered fields show where the most substantial changes had occurred during the intervening ten years. These amalgamations were probably by private agreement. The fields in Datchworth were not the subject of Parliamentary enclosure until 1867 when a few remaining strips were exchanged for pieces of land.[7]

Population of Datchworth in the early eighteenth century

The five surviving Window Tax returns from 1715 to 1735 indicate that the number of dwellings ranged between 33 and 37.[8] Information about exemptions and evasions is unknown, making this tax unreliable as a means of estimating population figures. A better source is that of the diocesan visitation records from Lincoln (1706-21) and London (1723-48). These give an estimate of 60 families residing in Datchworth during the first quarter of the eighteenth century. Using the recommended multiplier of 4.75, a population of about 285 is reached.[9]

---

[6] The strips in the open fields are dotted as in the original 1839 survey
[7] HALS: DP/33/26/1
[8] HALS: Land Tax, Datchworth, miscellaneous part contains window tax returns.
[9] L Munby, *Hertfordshire Population Statistics 1563-1801,* (Hertfordshire Local History Council 1964), pp9, 15, 32

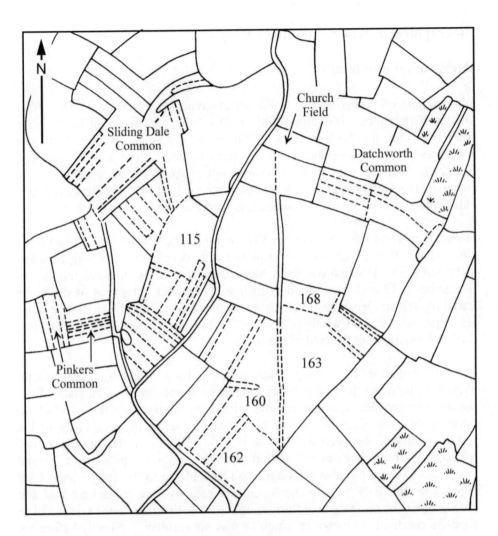

Figure 3
Remains of open fields in Datchworth in 1839 (HALS: DSA/4/34/2)

INTRODUCTION

Biographical notes on William Hawtayne

Background and family

William, son of Catherine and William Hawtayne, was born on 21 December 1680 at Farthinghoe (Northamptonshire). His father was rector of Farthinghoe from 1684 until his death in 1694. William had a younger brother, John, and five sisters.[10] On 2 December 1708, he married Anne Colebeck at St Anne and St Agnes, Aldersgate, London. Confirmation of Anne's maiden name can be found in the Datchworth Parish Register where in 1740, the burial of Mrs Hawtayne's mother, Elizabeth Colebeck is recorded aged 85 years.[11]

His early married life was spent at Elstree, where he was rector and had been since 1706. It was here that one son and four daughters were born between 1711 and 1716. His first daughter, Mary, died aged about eighteen months, in September 1713 and was buried at Elstree.[12] Another entry was made in the burial register in December 1710 recording the death of his 'Dear Brother John Hawtayne who was a Captain of Foot in Her Majesty Queen Anne her Service, died at Amsterdam in Holland of the small pox'.

From 1709 until 1718 Hawtayne was rector at both Elstree and Datchworth. Travelling between the two parishes cannot have been easy. The state of the roads in Hertfordshire could be terrible, with many 'sloughs and holes, which no horse could wade through', according to Daniel Defoe, in his account of his travels published between 1724 and 1727.[13] However, the installation of tollgates, or 'turnpikes', at this period provided gradual improvement in road conditions.[14] As a pluralist Hawtayne had to conform to the 1604 Canon Law stipulating that only two livings could be held by one incumbent and the parishes must be no more than thirty miles apart.[15] In addition, the rector had to supply a curate in the parish in which he was not resident.[16] Shortly before his

---

[10] J Foster (ed.) *Alumni Oxonienses 1500-1714*, (Oxford, 1891), vol II, p678; IGI

[11] HALS: DP/33/1/2

[12] HALS: DP/36/1/1

[13] D Defoe, *A Tour through England and Wales*, (Everyman's Library,1928), vol 2, p123

[14] P Hindle, *Roads and Tracks for Historians*, (Sussex, 2001), p92

[15] pluralist: one who holds two or more benefices simultaneously (J Richardson, *The Local Historian's Encyclopedia,*(1986) p191)

[16] A T Hart, *The Country Priest in English History,* (1959), pp118-119

induction, Hawtayne promised to keep a curate at Datchworth at a stipend of £30 per annum.[17] John Reynolds, Rector of Thorley paid his curate £30 a year in 1725, and in Warley (Essex) curates' stipends in the eighteenth century were said to be £30 per year and in the nineteenth century, £75 per year, suggesting that £30 per annum may have been a regional standard in the eighteenth century.[18] Datchworth and Elstree are roughly 19 miles apart, well within the statutory distance and there are several notes in Datchworth records alluding to curates (discussed below).

On 16 April 1719, Richard Bainbrigge succeeded to the living at Elstree following Hawtayne's resignation, so it may be assumed that the Hawtayne family moved to Datchworth sometime in late 1718 or early 1719.[19] By this time the family consisted of the remaining three daughters, Ann, Catherine and Elizabeth, and one son, William. Having left Elstree, Hawtayne became vicar of Shephall until 1733, a parish adjacent to Datchworth, where, of course, he was still rector. The Hawtaynes had one more daughter, Anna Margaretta, who was baptised at Shephall on 7 September 1720, about a month after the death of their eldest daughter Ann, who was buried at Datchworth.[20]

In 1733 for reasons unknown, he became vicar of All Saints, Leighton Buzzard (Bedfordshire) until his death. Investigations in the Leighton Buzzard parish records at Bedford have revealed that Hawtayne was an absentee vicar and visited on rare occasions, usually at the end of the year in March. It was then (from 1736 to 1746) that he signed his name at the end of the records of baptisms and burials for the preceding year.[21] This annual visit coincided with the receipt of a payment of 10s to the vicar, provided he delivered a sermon on 24 March, the end of the church year.[22] As explained in a Leighton Buzzard terrier dated 1709, this was one of three bequests of 10s. There were also two bequests of 20s and another one of 9s. Each bequest was in return for a sermon to be preached on a particular day such as Ascension Day, Good Friday or 1

---

[17] CCED, www.theclergydatabase.org.uk , accessed 12 September 2009

[18] HALS: DP/108/3/2; W R Powell (ed) *VCH, A History of the County of Essex,* (1978), vol 7, pp174-180, online, www.british-history.ac.uk , accessed 12 September 2009

[19] J E Cussans, *History of Hertfordshire,* (Originally published 1870-81, reprinted Yorkshire 1972), vol III, p83

[20] HALS: DP/100/1/1, DP/33/1/2

[21] BLARS: P91/1/2

[22] W Page (ed), *VCH, A History of the County of Bedfordshire,* (1912), vol III, pp399-417

INTRODUCTION

May. Hawtayne might have benefited from any of these, though there is no evidence that he did, but he could not have received the annual payment of £20 for reading divine service every morning in Leighton Buzzard church.[23]

The Hawtaynes' connection with Leighton Buzzard must have been more binding than the impression created so far. The parish register reveals that their daughter Elizabeth was married to the Reverend Samuel Clarke in October 1735 in Leighton Buzzard, however, there was no suggestion in the register that her father officiated at the wedding. Also, the burial of Anna M Hawtayne is recorded on 21 December 1803. She was almost certainly Anna Margaretta mentioned above.[24] It also appears that links with Elstree were not entirely severed. A Reverend Samuel Clarke became rector there on 25 September 1740. This man may have been the Hawtaynes' son-in-law, although there is no evidence to substantiate this. However, what is certain is that the next incumbent was Hawtayne's grandson, another William, who was at Elstree from 1787 until 1822.[25]

William Hawtayne died in Datchworth on 2 January 1748 aged 67. A memorial tablet is mounted on the north wall of the chancel in Datchworth church. The Latin inscription may be translated thus:

Here lie the remains of William Hawtayne MA who, always mindful of the poor and a despiser of riches, conscientiously exercised his pastoral ministry in the parish for 39 years. From this life of troubles he passed to the life of blessedness. Jan: 2 nd 1747 [1747/8].[26] Aged 69.

Hawtayne's age, as depicted on the tablet, is somewhat at odds with his date of birth, 21 December 1680; but whoever had the tablet inscribed may not have known exactly when he was born. His widow died on 29 June 1754. His son, William, made a great effort to get to grips with the parish tithe collection after his father's death and his handwriting is to be seen on the last few pages of the account book, ([66-70]). In 1749, not long after the death of his father, William was married at St Martin-in-the-Fields (London) but no other details have been

---

[23] BLARS: CRT 170/2/15/2

[24] BLARS: Bedfordshire Parish register Series, vols 31-33

[25] Cussans, *History of Hertfordshire*, vol III, p83

[26] 1747 would have been in the 'Old Style' calendar before the adoption of the Gregorian calendar in 1752.

'Datchworth Parsonage',
drawing by H G Oldfield, c 1800 (HALS: DE/Od/2, p495)

Photograph of the rectory taken before it was burnt down
in August 1977 (Datchworth Museum)

The Manor House Datchworth Herts
usually called Datchworth Bury

'The Manor House, Datchworth, Herts, usually called Datchworth Bury',
drawing by H G Oldfield, c 1800 (HALS: DE/Od/2, p497)
Built in 1728, according to the plaque, this manor house was demolished c 1860.

South-east view of Datchworth church with Datchworthbury in the background.
Drawing by J C Buckler, c 1835-40 (HALS: DE/Bg/4/155)

HIC
jacent Exuviæ
GULIELMI HAWTAYNE A.M
Qui, Pauperum semper Memor,
Divitiarum Contemptor,
In hac Parochiâ triginta et novem Annos
Pastoralem Diligenter
Egit Curam.
Ex hac Molestifsimâ, in Vitam
Beatifsimam Demigravit
Jan: 2° 1747
Ætat. 69.

Memorial tablet to William Hawtayne mounted on the north wall of the chancel of Datchworth church. The Latin inscription may be translated as follows:

Here lie the remains of William Hawtayne MA,
who, always mindful of the poor and a despiser of riches,
conscientiously exercised his pastoral ministry in the parish for 39 years.
From this life of troubles he passed to the life of blessedness
Jan: 2nd 1747 [1747/8]. Aged 69.

found about him except that his son, William, became Rector of Elstree in 1787.[27]

Education and career

William Hawtayne passed his childhood and teenage years during a time of considerable religious and political upheaval, due to a succession of monarchs. Charles II, who was on the throne when Hawtayne was born in 1680, died five years later and was succeeded by his brother James, as Charles had no legitimate heirs. James was a Catholic and his attempts to return the religion of England to Catholicism alienated much of the population. National anxiety was such that William of Orange was invited to come to England with an army to drive out James II. When William arrived in November 1688 he was met by an army that was unwilling to support James, who then fled to France. In February 1689, William and his Protestant wife, Mary (the eldest daughter of James), were declared king and queen of England. In 1694, aged 32, Mary died childless, and William died in 1702, the year after the Act of Settlement that banned Catholics from the throne. Anne, James II's youngest daughter, succeeded. As Hawtayne grew up he must have been increasingly aware of these national events both during his education at Rugby and as a student at Trinity College, Oxford, whence he graduated BA in 1701. He later graduated MA from King's College, Cambridge, in 1707.

Hawtayne's professional life began in Peterborough where he was ordained deacon on 20 September 1702 and then priest on 19 December 1703. Thenceforward, the strands of Hawtayne's clerical career developed in several directions commencing at Elstree and holding the living at Datchworth in parallel as observed earlier. Meanwhile, he became Army Chaplain to a regiment of Welsh fusiliers in Germany and Flanders.[28] The exact period of this particular commitment is not known, but, assuming that the need for troops in this region was caused by the War of the Spanish Succession, it was sometime before 1713. He was also chaplain to the Earl of Essex in 1709, according to a Datchworth Parish Register entry (below), where he recorded his induction into Datchworth Rectory after the death of his predecessor John Gaile.[29]

---

[27] IGI
[28] J & J A Venn, *Alumni Cantabrigienses*, (Cambridge, 1922), vol II, p338
[29] HALS: DP/33/1/2

INTRODUCTION

John Gaile a Native of France, But Rector of this Parish by Presentation of Elizabeth Countesse Dow[age]r of Essex by having travailed with her son Algernoon [*sic*] Earl of Essex into Italy,[30] dyed at Brusselles in Flanders in Sept[embe]r 1709 and was then succeeded by William Hawtayne \A.M/[31] then Chaplain to Algernoon Earl of Essex but at his Request presented by his Mother Elizabeth Countesse Dowager of Essex. William Hawtayne was then Rector of the Parish of Idilstree alias Ellstree in this County and in the Liberty of St Albans which he Exchang'd for the Vicaridge of Sheephall afterwards in the Year 1718. Teste Memore Meo [*sic*][*my memory as witness*] Gul[ielmu]s Hawtayne

In addition, George I's daughter-in-law, Caroline of Ansbach, who was said to have been particularly interested in theological matters, engaged Hawtayne as her chaplain, probably soon after George I's accession to the throne in 1714.[32] Mention is made of this appointment at the assize sermon of July 16 1716.[33] Hawtayne kept this position until she became Queen in 1727.[34] The quoted entry from the Datchworth Parish Register mentions the parish of Shephall for which he took responsibility, as vicar, until 1733. Unusually, Shephall vicarage was endowed with great tithes, as noted by Salmon.[35] Shephall parish is north-east of Datchworth in a detached part of Cashio Hundred. The main part of Cashio Hundred is in south-west Hertfordshire in which Elstree lies and, indeed, Cassiobury (Watford), one of the Essex family seats. These links with the Essex family are not reflected in the patronage of either the Shephall or Elstree

---

[30] Gaile was Algernon's tutor. He was a layman, but the Countess obtained dispensation for him and he assumed priest's orders. He was presented to Datchworth in 1694. (T O Beachcroft and W B Emms, *Five Hide Village*, (Datchworth Parish Council, 1984) p59)
[31] *Artium Magister*, Master of Arts
[32] J H Plumb, *The Four Georges*, (1956), p44
[33] *A Sermon Preach'd at the Assizes at Hertford July 16 1716. Before the Right Honourable the Lord Chief Justice Parker and Sir Littleton Powis Knight one of the Judges of the King's Bench.* By William Hawtayne M A Rector of Da[t]chworth in the County of Hertford. (London Printed for R Burleigh in Amen-Corner MDCCXIV, price four pence), p1
[34] Foster (ed) *Alumni Oxonienses*, vol II, p678
[35] 'This vicarage was at the Dissolution endowed with the Great Tythes, and though nothing appears, we may presume it was at the Desire of Mr Nodes [*the impropriator who was formerly a tenant to the Abbot of St Albans Abbey*] who might have had the impropriation if he would' (N Salmon, *The History of Hertfordshire Describing the County and its Antient Monuments*, (1728), pp198, 199)

advowson, unlike Datchworth where the Dowager Countess of Essex was patron at the time of Hawtayne's induction.

Sermons

Hawtayne must have been well thought of, as he was asked to preach several significant sermons that were published soon after. Two of the three surviving sermons have been selected for discussion below.

Thanksgiving for George I's accession to the throne

Queen Anne's death, on 1 August 1714, marked the end of 'a time of waiting' for Jacobites. They became particularly active during the early years of George I's reign, commencing with riots in the streets on Coronation Day, 20 October 1714.[36] The first of Hawtayne's published sermons, dated 20 January 1715, was preached at Elstree on the day of thanksgiving for King George's accession to the throne, (dedicated to Her Royal Highness the Princess of Wales).[37] The date is significant as it was a few days before a parliamentary election in which one of the candidates was Charles Caesar of Benington, an alleged Jacobite.[38] It was a long sermon outlining George's lineage and attempting to reassure the congregation of his suitability to be king. He represented 'a Deliverence from a *French* King, a *French* Government and a *French* Religion; all which must inevitably have been our Lot, had not Providence in Mercy saved us from it, by making us happy in His Majesty's mild and gracious Government'.[39] Later Hawtayne refers to the king's 'Piety towards Man ... How great and kind was the Concern he expressed upon those unhappy Accidents, which fell out on the Day of his Coronation?' This was probably referring to the Jacobite riots that took place on the day. This theme carried on throughout, ending on the following note:

---

[36] L M Munby, *The common people are not nothing, conflict in religion and politics in Hertfordshire, 1575-1780,* (Hertfordshire, 1995), pp98-100

[37] *A Sermon Preach'd at Elstree in Hertfordshire, on the Twentieth of January, 1714 [1714/15]. Being the Day of Thanksgiving to Almighty God for His Majesty King George's Safe Arrival and Peaceable Accession to the Throne of these Kingdoms.* By William Hawtayne, A M Rector of the said Parish. (London: Printed for Tim. Goodwin, at the Queen's Head against St Dunstan's Church in Fleetstreet. 1714, price 3d).

[38] J Oates, 'Hertfordshire and the Jacobite Rebellions of 1715 and 1745', *Herts Past & Present,* 3rd series, (Spring 2004), p3

[39] *A Sermon Preach'd at Elstree,* p7

INTRODUCTION

We had a very great escape at the Revolution, effected by King *William* of ever Blessed and Glorious Memory; he stept in but just timely for a Relief. But the best effects of that Undertaking were for a long Time prevented, and very often hazarded by a Sett of restless and ungrateful Persons, ... many of them openly aiming at the Restoration of the Pretender and Popery. ... By these very Men was his present Majesty's Succession brought in very great Danger: By them is his Person reviled, and so is the Prince, the Princess, and their whole Family, as well their Glorious Ancestors, as their Royal Infants, in the most insolent and abusive manner. I blush, my Brethren, for my Countrymen and Fellow Citizens in speaking of it; but I know myself, that they are treated by some persons amongst us with more Rudeness and Scurrility, than People of good Sense, or good Manners, and common Humanity, would treat the poorest Beggar upon the Dunghill. Oh Shameful!...

Let us according to our Duty, believe well of our King, till he gives us just Reason to believe otherwise of him.[40]

Hertford Assize sermon, July 1716

Hawtayne's second published sermon was delivered at the opening of the Hertford summer assizes in 1716.[41] Assizes were trials before a jury and, from the thirteenth century, were presided over by itinerant 'justices of the assize' who travelled from London. By 1337, counties of England were divided into six circuits each under the responsibility of particular judges and there were usually two visitations a year. The 'Home' circuit, to which Hertfordshire belonged, also included Essex, Kent, Middlesex, Surrey and Sussex. Deciding where in the county the court sessions should be held took years to refine and became somewhat competitive between towns that had gaols, each wanting to avoid the inconvenient business of transporting prisoners from their gaol to the courthouse in a distant town. Hertford Castle was the main venue for Hertfordshire assizes until 1610, apart from occasional visits to St Albans, Bishop's Stortford or Hitchin. Soon after, assizes were held at the Sessions House that stood on the present site of Shire Hall and would have been in use in Hawtayne's time.[42]

---

[40] *A Sermon Preach'd at Elstree*, p16

[41] Notes about assizes that follow, have been made using J S Cockburn's *A history of English assizes 1558-1714* as the principal source.

[42] C Heath, 'Pride and Justice, Pomp and Pleasure, A Social History' in *The Restoration of Shire Hall Hertford*, (Hertfordshire County Architects, 1990), pp45, 46

INTRODUCTION

Judges were selected in February and July each year with the condition that they did not ride circuits in counties where they resided.[43]

On their arrival at the county boundary, the two chosen judges were met by the sheriff, local officials and gentry, all accompanied by trumpeters, contributing towards a great spectacle of pomp and ceremony. After the judges had been to their lodgings, they were taken to the parish church where the formal proceedings commenced with a sermon delivered by the sheriff's chaplain. The assize sermon was often printed and, as such, was likely to reach a larger audience than the immediate congregation to whom it had been delivered. For this reason, the sheriff chose his chaplain carefully, ideally with the approval of the bishop, to avoid any likelihood of political controversy arising from the content of his sermon. Sometimes it was found necessary to engage a court chaplain or an incumbent resident in London to perform this duty.[44] Hawtayne, as chaplain to Princess Caroline, had the right credentials.

His sermon was delivered at the Assizes at Hertford on 16 July 1716, in the presence of Lord Chief Justice Parker, Sir Littleton Powis, John Duncombe Esq, High Sheriff of the County of Hertford, and, of course, the gentlemen of the jury. It was printed at the request of the High Sheriff and sold for 4d. Such topics as tolerance, suffering, laws and appropriate punishments were frequently chosen for the assize sermon, being considered free from contention. Hawtayne selected the theme of hypocrisy for his sermon, using the text, Romans II, 3: 'And thinkest thou this, O Man, that judgest, and dost the same, that thou shalt escape the Judgement of God?'.[45] Towards the end of his sermon of about 6000 words, he managed, once again, to upbraid certain members of the church for their 'present Behaviour ... who so scandalously prevaricate with God and Man in the Matter of Oaths; who will tell you, with a bare Face, that they swear with the Tongue, but not with the Heart; and who, notwithstanding their Oaths to the King, think themselves at liberty to give their Wishes to the Pretender'.[46]

Considering the political tone of these two sermons it is perhaps surprising to learn that in the 1722 parliamentary election, Hawtayne voted for Charles Caesar of Benington, a Jacobite, and Ralph Freeman of Braughing, Caesar's

---

[43] J S Cockburn, *A history of English assizes 1558-1714*, (Cambridge, 1972), pp17, 19, 20, 23, 27, 49

[44] Cockburn, *A history of English assizes*, pp65-66

[45] *A Sermon Preach'd at the Assizes at Hertford*, p5

[46] *A Sermon Preach'd at the Assizes at Hertford*, p27

brother-in-law.[47] These two candidates both resided in eastern Hertfordshire and so may have been geographically more attractive, whereas Thomas Sebright, the third candidate, lived in Flamstead, some distance to the west. Of greater significance may be that 20 out of the 22 votes cast in Datchworth were for Caesar, including that of Edward Harrison of Balls Park, who, by then, owned Datchworthbury Manor, and was an enthusiastic supporter of Caesar.[48] However, in the subsequent elections of 1727 and 1734, despite Datchworth's continued support for Caesar, Hawtayne was part of the minority that did not vote for him.

Tithes
Historical background

An account of the history of tithes would be incomplete without the provision of the biblical references that caused so much heartache in their interpretation. A few examples are worth quoting. Jacob vowed: 'And all that thou shalt give me I will surely give the tenth unto thee' (Genesis, 28:22). In the law of Moses: 'And all the tithe of the land, whether of the seed of the land, or the fruit of the tree, is the Lord's: and the tithe of the herd, or the flock, even of whatsoever passeth under the rod, the tenth shall be holy unto the Lord.'[49] (Leviticus, 27:30-32). This sounds fairly straightforward as a principle until a few questions are asked: What was to be tithed? Who had to pay? To whom were the tithes paid? What would they be used for? The two principal sources that have been used in trying to unravel these mysteries are *A History of Tithes* by Henry William Clarke, first published in 1891, and 'Monastic Tithes from their Origin to the Twelfth Century' by Giles Constable, published in 1964.

It seems that, initially, the payment of tithes was confined to the Jews in Jerusalem until the Roman destruction of the second temple in AD 70. Something similar to tithes, relating to the spoils of war, was paid by the Greeks to Apollo and by the Romans to Hercules. According to Clarke, nothing is written about tithes in the first and second centuries and only exhortations were issued in the third and fourth centuries, which became more forceful from the fifth century. One of the earliest recorded messages pertaining to tithes, and,

---

[47] Munby, *The common people*, pp95, 118; HALS: QPE 6-12, Datchworth poll books
[48] Munby, *The common people*, p122
[49] It was customary for a shepherd to mark every tenth sheep with a coloured rod as they were released from a sheep pen (H W Clarke, *A History of Tithes*, (1894), pp1-2)

incidentally, to the moral obligation to pay, was delivered in a sermon by Caesarius of Arles, where he was bishop from 503-542. In it he said that tithes should be paid 'for the sake not of God who receives them but of those who pay them, whose eternal salvation depends upon faithful payment'. He had the view that all talents should be tithed, and that could mean anything that contributed to the source of one's livelihood, including, for example, military service and the products of business or trade, as well as the fruits of agriculture, which eventually became the sole source of tithes. An interesting view was proposed by Pope Gregory (590-604) concerning the forty days of fasting during Lent. He was not alone in suggesting that they should be treated as the tithe of one's time being roughly a tenth of a year.[50] It was firmly believed that everyone had to pay tithes, even the clergy, but since the church was the obvious recipient of tithes, in that they were meant to be paid to the Lord, it seemed unnecessary for the clergy to conform, and so those with ecclesiastical responsibilities either put their tithes to clerical use or were exempt. Some lenience was also extended to the very poor, who were not forced to pay.

As Christianity spread westwards, so did the custom of paying tithes. By the fifth and sixth centuries the practice was well established in parts of France, Italy, Spain and part of what is now Austria. Augustine, the first Archbishop of Canterbury, brought Christianity to Britain in 597 but the custom of tithing took time to become established. After his death in 604, the next Archbishop of Canterbury to make any significant impression was Theodore of Tarsus, the Greek theologian, who was appointed to the see in 668. Recognised as being one of the most learned churchmen of his time, he restructured the diocesan system and united the churches of the separate Anglo-Saxon kingdoms. Formalising tithing practice was probably part of this procedure, and mention was made in Theodore's second Penitential (c 686). As such, this is the earliest known reference to tithes in England.[51]

Some monasteries existed before 597, but the arrival of Augustine at Canterbury marked the beginning of an era of monastery and abbey construction, starting with Canterbury Cathedral. During the seventh century, monks set forth to spread the gospel, necessitating the establishment of regional monasteries called 'minsters'. At the same time, Theodore encouraged the building of churches on large estates to overcome the difficulties encountered by remote worshippers

---

[50] G Constable, 'Monastic Tithes from their Origin to the Twelfth Century', *Cambridge Studies in Medieval Life and Thought*, new series, X, (1964), p18

[51] Clarke, *A History of Tithes*, pp20-21

when trying to reach the nearest minster, or, as it was sometimes called, the 'mother church'. The landowners could appoint a priest to officiate in the new church and he was provided with a house and some land. This land, called the glebe, varied from 'five acres to a hide or more'.[52] At this stage, tithes were paid to the mother church.

Constable has observed that during this period the distinction between religious and secular obligation was narrow, and though no law existed, the sense of duty adopted by many Christians to pay tithes was profound.[53] Nevertheless, legalisation was sought and Charlemagne was the first to introduce civil enforcement in 779. In essence it was confirmation of current practice but had the means for people outside the church to help clergy in their collection of tithes, by using built in penalties for not paying.[54] These included exclusion from the church, demands for fines, the closing of the guilty party's house and ultimately, imprisonment.[55]

In 787 papal legates were sent from Rome to England where they had meetings in the kingdoms of Mercia and Northumbria. Tithes in these kingdoms alone received 'legal sanction', but, as there was no means of enforcing this 'law', it was not legally binding. There followed what Clarke describes as a period of 'dead silence', a time in which England suffered Danish invasions.[56] Amid the plundering of churches and monasteries many written historical records were destroyed, so any developments in the system of tithing that may have taken place at that time have failed to survive.[57] It was not until 960 that the legal compulsion to pay tithes in England was enforced by Edgar. Once tithes were legally binding, their implementation had to be clarified taking custom into consideration. All had to pay, but priests were usually exempt and the poor were not forced into paying. It was also the case that tithes were paid on produce and service; ideas alluded to by Caesarius of Arles in the sixth century. Who, then, should be the recipients?

Opinions varied and were the subject of discussion between European theologians, often by letter. Some suggested that payment should be in return

---

[52] Clarke, *A History of Tithes,* pp21-26
[53] Constable, 'Monastic Tithes', p24
[54] Constable, 'Monastic Tithes', p29
[55] Clarke, *A History of Tithes,* p34
[56] Clarke, *A History of Tithes,* pp43-46
[57] A Savage, *The Anglo-Saxon Chronicles,*(2002), p90

INTRODUCTION

for the sacraments, others that tithes should be paid to the church where baptism had been administered. The latter view provided some protection for the baptismal church against the threat of a new church that may have been built nearby laying claim to tithes.[58]

In an attempt to overcome this problem, an early ninth century statute stated that 'every church should have the boundary of the estates from which it receives the tithes'.[59] Some felt that this policy was too rigid and, in 895, at the Council of Tribur (Germany), a compromise was agreed that if a church was built four or five miles away from the older church, then, with the consent of the bishop, the landowner could appoint a priest and collect the new tithe.[60] There are elements in this agreement that echo Theodore's ideas in England 200 years earlier.

In 960 Edgar detailed his version of compromise differently. The mother church had the right to the tithes of a particular estate, but, if another church on the estate had a burial ground, the priest in charge had the right to one third of the tithes, the remaining two thirds went to the mother church. However, as time went on, and probably as the old minsters declined, the destination of the two thirds share was variable according to the whim of the landowner and in many cases went to the estate church.[61] If there was no burial ground, the landowner took the tithes and provided for the priest as he saw fit, out of his own pocket.[62]

After 1066, the Normans made sweeping changes to the existing arrangements. New monasteries were built in great numbers, the twelfth century alone accounted for over 300. Many Saxon churches were rebuilt in stone. Norman successors to original patrons appropriated their churches to the regional monastery. Associated with each church were the glebe and tithes that together constituted the 'rectory'.[63] These, with the advowson,[64] were acquired by the monastery and so, automatically, the monastery appointed itself as rector. The lands that went with these churches were the origins of parishes as we know

---

[58] Constable, 'Monastic Tithes', pp36-37
[59] Constable, 'Monastic Tithes', p38
[60] Constable, 'Monastic Tithes', p41
[61] Clarke, *A History of Tithes,* p93
[62] Lord Ernle, *English Farming Past and Present,* (1927), p336
[63] www.practicalconveyancing.co.uk/content/view/10231/1132 accessed 16 Feb 2009
[64] advowson: the right of a patron or institution to appoint a priest to a living to care for the souls in the local population

INTRODUCTION

them today.[65] About a fifth of English parishes had undergone the process of appropriation by c1200, and nearly half by the end of the Middle Ages.[66] The monastery, in its position as rector, had the responsibility to administer to the spiritual needs of the church congregation and to ensure that the chancel of the church was properly maintained. Also, according to the 1391 Statute of Mortmain, each monastic institution was ordered to reserve a proportion of its income for poor relief.[67] In practice, the church so appropriated was often too far from the monastery for a monk to supply the cure, so a vicar was appointed as a substitute. In the early days, the vicar was given a stipend, an amount that could be variable and arbitrary. Later, to augment what was often a small allowance, vicars were given the right to the small tithes.[68]

Under the Third Lateran Council of 1179, it was decreed that appropriations could no longer be made without the consent of the bishop. The matter of tithes was not properly clarified until the Fourth Lateran Council of 1215. Thenceforward, tithes that had hitherto been given by the landowners to any church of their choice had to be given to the incumbent. Tithes that had belonged to the resident priest before 1215 could not be appropriated and tithes that had been appropriated to institutions outside the parish continued to be so.[69]

The final matter for consideration concerns the practical use of tithes. After collection by the clergy, the distribution of tithes had to be decided. This was another question filled with controversy that lasted throughout the Carolingian period (751-987). Benefactors were combinations of the poor, the bishop, the clergy, pilgrims and the fabric of the church itself. In England, a system of tripartition was adopted that shared the income between the poor, the church fabric and the priests, a method that survived until the eleventh century.[70]

The Dissolution of the Monasteries, from 1536 to 1540, created a major upheaval. As monasteries were destroyed the rectorial endowments went to the Crown and subsequently were sold or granted to lay rectors. These, according to Ernle, were given the title of 'impropriators' to distinguish them from the spiritual nature of the original appropriators or, as Clarke suggests, they were

---

[65] J A Venn, *Foundations of Agricultural Economics*, (Cambridge, 1933), p151
[66] K Tiller, *English Local History: an Introduction*, (Gloucestershire, 2002), pp69,71
[67] W E Tate, *The Parish Chest*, (Cambridge, 1969), p190
[68] Ernle, *English Farming*, p340
[69] Clarke, *A History of Tithes,* pp148-151
[70] Constable, 'Monastic Tithes', p56

named thus because they were improper persons.[71] Whoever owned the rectorial property benefited from tithes but had the burden of the chancel maintenance. The incumbent of the associated parish church still received the vicarial tithes. A glebe terrier, written by the vicar of Newnham in 1637, alludes to these matters in the section devoted to tithes: 'all Tithes except corne, hay & hempe[72] which was pay'd formerly to the last Incumbents but is now datayned by the Impropriator'.[73] Disruptions during the Civil Wars threatened the system of tithing. Several thousand incumbents were evicted and replaced by nonconformist ministers who were not always popular among the parishioners, many of whom refused to pay tithes, secretly giving financial support to the ejected rector or vicar. There was a move to abandon tithing altogether but Parliament acknowledged that the system was the simplest way of financing the clergy and so it continued.[74] At the Restoration, parishes recovered slowly from the disruptions, but some may have suffered permanently.

The nature of tithes

Tithes were originally in three categories. First, the predial tithes payable on all things arising from the ground, such as wood, hay, corn and other crops; all could be harvested and regenerated annually. Secondly, mixed tithes for things that were the products of animal husbandry, such as calves, lambs and also, milk, wool and eggs. The word 'mixed' in this context meant that tithes were related to stock and labour combined.[75] Finally, putting into practice the laws of King Edgar, men's labours had to be tithed on, for example, their profits in the mill or at the fishery. This personal tithe, as it was called, was the most difficult to administer and was effectively abolished in 1549. Fallow land and glebe-land in the occupation of the incumbent were exempt from tithe payments.[76]

The resident rector collected all tithes and the distinction between different categories of tithe only became significant when the living was held by an absentee rector or an institution. In this latter case, a vicar was appointed to perform parochial duties. In this context, tithes were divided into 'great' and

---

[71] Ernle, *English Farming*, p340; Clarke, *A History of Tithes,* p160
[72] hemp was used to make rough cloth, ropes and sacking (J Bristow, *The Local Historian's Glossary & Vade Mecum* (Nottingham, 1997), p96
[73] HALS: ASA/3/1
[74] Hart, *The Country Priest,* pp114, 117-18
[75] S Friar, *The Local History Companion,* (Stroud, 2001), p436
[76] J P Kain and H C Prince, *Tithe Surveys for Historians,* (2000), p3

'small'. The great tithe was almost synonymous with the predial tithe, but applied specifically to hay, corn and wood, though this was not a strict rule and was subject to regional custom. All other crops and produce came under the heading of small tithes, sometimes called 'privy' tithes. Sir Simon Degge, in his efforts to advise clergy on the complexities of tithing rules, illustrates the power of custom in overcoming a doubtful situation:

> But there has been some question whether Tithe Wood should be accounted a great or minute Tithe, and resolved, that if a Vicar be only endowed with the small Tithes, and have by reason thereof always had Tithe Wood, that in such Case it shall be accounted a small Tithe, otherwise it is to be accounted amongst the great Tithes.[77]

An example of a vicar benefiting from tithe wood is to be found in the early 1700s in Sawbridgeworth.[78] An acre of wood was sold for £5, in another location 3½ acres realised £30, and finally 5 acres and 15 poles fetched £15, making a total of £50, for which the tithe of £5 was paid.[79] The variation of value in the wood sold is of interest but unfortunately the types of wood are not given. The final entry at Sawbridgeworth relates to wood received in kind. It states: 'Felled … 6 acre 3 roods & 3 poles. Rec[eive]d in kind 2 roods 6 pole ½ value £3 4s 10½d'. This latter amount was slightly under one tenth of the wood felled and generated a tithe of about £6 per acre, which was close to the average for the wood sold above.

Collection of tithes: in kind

Historically, tithes were collected in kind, a practice fraught with difficulties and frustrations for both payer and collector. To illustrate these characteristics some of the more common commodities have been singled out below.

Crops

In the case of crops of hay and corn, every tenth haycock or stook of corn had to be 'separated' for inspection by the rector at a pre-arranged time. Only then could the farmer remove his own share of the crop. The rector was now the owner of the selected tithes and was responsible for arranging collection and carriage by his tithing men who, then, might take the produce directly to a tithe

---

[77] Sir S Degge, *The Parson's Counsellor with the Law of Tithes or Tithing* (1676) p144
[78] HALS: DP/98/3/3
[79] 1 acre = 4 roods, 1 rood = 40 poles, 1 pole = 30¼ square yards

barn for storage.[80] A tardy rector could make life difficult for the farmer who was eager to use the land for grazing cattle or to plough it in preparation for the next crop.[81] Each farmer would have been one of many waiting for the parson's visit, all of whom would be hoping to get in their crop before a sudden change to bad weather, adding stress to an already anxious time. Tithes were an important part of the parson's livelihood, but set against this was the expense of hiring men, carts and horses, so although it was in his interests to be an efficient collector, it may well have cost him more to be so.

Some parsons incurred even more expense by resorting to litigation to resolve disputes arising from such arrangements as described above. There was a case (as late as 1783) in Walkern where the rector had a dispute with his parish about the time of setting out the hay and corn. The questions put to a Lincolns Inn lawyer suggest that the rector may have been new to the parish and unlucky enough not to have inherited tithing instructions from the previous incumbent. The questions and replies are below.[82]

> What Quantity of Hay & Grain etc is the Farmer obliged to set out at once for the Rector or Tythingman?
> Is the Rector obliged to tithe any <u>small Quantities</u> which may be set out as often as the Farmer thinks proper to send to him?
>
> [*Reply*] If the field in w[hi]ch the Corn or Grass grows is of moderate size, & is all ripe at the same time, & no accid[en]t from weather [&c], prevents the farmer from cutt[ing] the whole field with[ou]t interruption, he ought to reap or cut the whole crop & set out the Tyth of the whole before he removes any part of the Crop. The Question, if disputed, will depend on the Farmer acting *bona fide* or *mala fide*.
>
> Can the Farmer remove any Hay or Grain from the Field before he has sent notice to the parson & in consequence of such notice the Tythingman has attended; and what time is allowed for his attendance after such notice has been given?

---

[80] Not all large barns were necessarily tithe barns; some were built to store crops produced on a large estate (D Hey, *The Oxford Companion to Local and Family History*, (Oxford, 1996), p440)
[81] E J Evans, *The Contentious Tithe,*(1976), p23
[82] HALS: DP/114/3/9

INTRODUCTION

[*Reply*] Unless <u>the Custom of the Parish</u> requires notice to be given, previously to the Tyth being set out, no notice is necessary. All that the Common Law requires is, that after the farmer has set out his tyths the whole Crop, Tyths & all, sh[oul]d remain on the ground for such a reasonable time as to enable the Rector … to see that the Tyths are fairly set out.

When the Tithe is severed from the other nine parts, has not the Rector a Right to remove it as soon as he pleases without waiting for the Farmer?

[*Reply*] When the farmer shall have set out & distinguish[e]d the Tyths from the 9 parts, … the Rector … may carry away the Tyths.

The lawyer's guarded replies probably gave the rector the authority he wanted, but it was left to him to study the motives of his recalcitrant farmers ('*bone fide* or *mala fide*') and to investigate the 'custom' of the parish.

A more fortunate vicar of Willian, in 1828, inherited instructions about crops explaining that 'Wheat and Rye tythes need to be paid by the tenth Shock;[83] Barley, Oats, Peas, Beans and all other Corn by the tenth Cock[84] and Hay the same'.[85]

The new crop of turnips that was grown in the open fields from the late seventeenth century provided a fresh source of controversy in respect of its tithing.[86] If grown as a crop and taken from the ground, it was tithed in kind, but if left in the ground and used as fodder to fatten cattle, the amount might be based on the value of the land similar to grass grazed by barren or non-working cattle described below.[87] No tithe was due if grazing cows were in milk.

Hay was a valuable crop and the 'aftermath' was used for cattle grazing.[88] Hawtayne made reference to 'lattermarth hay' for which he collected tithe: this

---

[83] Shock, stook: several sheaves propped against each other (Bristow, *Glossary*, p178)
[84] cock: a small conical heap (Bristow, *Glossary*, p42)
[85] HALS: AHH/3/1
[86] D Hey *The Oxford Companion to Local and Family History*, (Oxford, 1996) p454
[87] E Evans, 'Tithes'in J Thirsk, (ed), *The agrarian history of England and Wales, 1640-1750*, vol V, (Cambridge 1985), p401
[88] aftermath: the new growth after the first hay harvest

was probably a second crop that was allowed to grow but was not used as pasture **[28]**.

Orchards and gardens

The produce of orchards was generally taken in kind. However, the parson of Furneaux Pelham had a system of setting up a 'composition' payment for a year then switching back to collecting in kind if the prospects of the orchard looked promising.[89] For example, in 1728, the parson compounded Thomas Parker's 'Orchard for failing' for 1s 6d. In October the same year the parson wrote 'I declar[e]d his composition [of 1s 6d] void upon the Orchard's being a very good one'.[90] In October 1729 he records 'By 2 Bush[els] & ½ of Apples, 2s 6d'. Though 1729 was a good year it was the last year the orchard was mentioned and in subsequent years Thomas Parker's only contributions were a matter of pence for 'eggs and offerings'.

Crops grown in gardens were subject to tithe but the produce was usually on such a small scale that going through the separation procedure to extract a tenth was not practical. An annual payment of a 'garden penny' was introduced to cover this particular tithe. A tithe book from Barley in 1738 contains regular entries annotated 'g.p.' and amounted to 6d rather than 1d.[91] The garden penny is often mentioned at the same time as the 'hearth penny' paid in lieu of firewood.

Cattle and sheep

The tithing of livestock would have been easy if lambs, calves, etc, always appeared in multiples of ten. As this event was most unlikely a system evolved that covered all eventualities. Taking the example of calves, if there were under seven, the parson took either ½d per calf or a tenth of its value if sold. He took one tithe calf if there were seven to ten calves and paid the farmer a halfpenny per calf 'found wanting' for ten. In 1633 Thomas Hassall of Amwell used this method for calves, and similarly for lambs, but, if there were fewer than seven, the custom there was to 'drive' the number forward to the next season until the number was high enough to take a tithe lamb, so effectively carrying over the account to the next year.[92] This practice must have been sufficiently common to

---

[89] composition: a form of tithe commutation agreed for a fixed period of time.

[90] HALS: DP/78/3/2

[91] HALS: DP/14/3/3

[92] S G Doree, (ed), *The parish and tithing book of Thomas Hassall of Amwell,* (HRS, Cambridge, 1989), pp208-209

invite the disapproval of Degge who wrote that this 'is not allowed by our Law, for Tithes must be paid annually' and in fact it was an unpopular custom.[93]

The choice of lambs was often governed by customary rules and the tithe instructions inherited by Hassall provide a good example. In Amwell the owner chose two lambs, then the parson selected one, the next seven were then the farmer's choice and so on.[94] This method was supposed to instil an element of fairness into the choice such that the parson was not left with the weakest lambs and the farmer did not lose his best ones.

The tithing of wool followed a similar pattern to that for calves: if there were seven fleeces, the parson would have one fleece and then he paid the farmer ½d for every fleece from the eighth to the tenth.[95]

Cattle, if used for the 'plough or pail' or for domestic consumption, were not tithed. However, in Granborough (Buckinghamshire), for a calf that was killed for the use of the owner, the left shoulder was due to the vicar.[96] For cattle that were barren or not working, then there was an agistment tithe of one tenth of the value of the pasture, paid by the owner of the grazed land.[97] As Anne Tarver explains, the grass thus consumed would otherwise have been allowed to grow and be cut as hay and subsequently tithed as such.[98]

Milk

Milk was notoriously difficult to deal with in kind. A common source of conflict was whether it should be collected by the parson or delivered to the church. The Walkern farmer, mentioned in the legal case above concerning grain and hay, also raised the matter of milk. He insisted that the rector should fetch the milk from the farm. He produced a witness whose husband was employed by the last rector but one, to fetch the milk for a short time. The rector had a witness 'who remembers meeting a person with milk from another farm, as he was carrying it to the Churchyard, in the time of a preceding Rector; and a second witness who remembers to have heard his Father say that the milk

---

[93] Degge, *The Parson's Counsellor*, p170; Doree, *Thomas Hassall of Amwell*, p xxxix
[94] Doree, *Thomas Hassall of Amwell*, p209
[95] A Tarver, *Church court records: an introduction for family and local historians*, (Chichester, 1995) p104
[96] HALS: ASA/3/1
[97] agistment: depasturing or grazing
[98] Tarver, *Church court records*, p102

was thrown down in the Churchyard, as the Rector's man was not there to receive it.' In reply to the main question: 'Is the Rector to fetch the Milk, or is it to be brought to the Churchyard?', the lawyer cited some cases in 1720 when milk had to be set out in the farmers' pails in the yard for collection. If the milk was not collected by next milking time, then the milk could be 'thrown on the ground for want of his pails'. He concluded that 'there scarcely seems evidence sufficient to suppose a custom of carrying the Milk Tythe to the Church Porch.'

In Granborough (Buckinghamshire), in 1707, it was stated clearly in a glebe terrier that milk was 'due in kind to be paid every Tenth day Evening and Morning beginning att Hock Monday[99] and Ending at Lamass day [*1 August*] Inclusive' then again from 'the Feast day of St Michaell the Archangell [*29 September*]'to 'St Martin's day Inclusive [*11 November*]'.[100]

Some parishes reached a compromise by either paying in milk, or in cheese made from milk, or partly milk and partly cheese, sometimes related to the seasons. However, many parishes found it more satisfactory to use a form of payment called a *modus* usually of ancient origin. Instead of the parson receiving milk in kind, the farmer paid him a fixed amount for each 'milch' cow, perhaps 1d or 2d, these amounts being reduced by a ½d for a stripped or dry cow, sometimes called a stropper.[101]

Other livestock
Foals, pigs and geese were often treated in the same way as lambs but sometimes for a small farm, it was more appropriate to pay a *modus* for each foal. In Fleckney (Leicestershire) in 1638, it was 1d, as it was in Laxton (Nottinghamshire) in 1714; whereas a *modus* in Brotherton (Yorkshire) stated that the tithe was 4d per foal.[102]

Bees were often tithed by the swarm but their produce of honey and wax were also a frequent way of tithing in kind. An example may be found in the Furneaux Pelham tithing book where 2½ lbs of honey and wax raised a tithe of

---

[99] Hock Monday: the second Monday after Easter Sunday (*OED*)
[100] HALS: ASA/3/1
[101] *modus*: a shortened form of *modus decimandi*, a customary fixed payment in lieu of tithing in kind (Bristow, *Glossary*, p133)
[102] Tarver, *Church court records*, p104; C S & C S Orwin, *The open fields* (Oxford 1967) p158; Venn, *Agricultural Economics*, p158

1s 6d in 1730.[103] Anne Tarver makes the point that, by the eighteenth century, imports of sugar and the making of candles from tallow caused such tithes to largely disappear.[104] This may have applied more to urban rather than rural areas.

In 1638, in Fleckney (Leicestershire), the tithe for a hen was two eggs and for a cockerel three eggs. The same rate pertained in Amwell until, at an unknown date, this method was commuted to payments of ½d for a hen and 1d for a cock. Pigeons were tithed if sold, but if used solely for family consumption, they were exempt.[105]

Collection of tithes: *Modus* and composition

Modus and composition payments have already been alluded to. There were two categories of *modus* payment and both had the characteristics of being fixed in the distant past and having long term status. The parochial sort, used throughout a particular parish, was related to payments in lieu of kind, such as 2d for a swarm of bees or half a crown for a dovecote, or perhaps, 2d per acre in lieu of the tithe of hay. The second type was a farm *modus* where an agreement had been made in possibly medieval times between the lord of the manor and the rector for a definite sum, such as the £2 12s 4d for 1,390 acres in Abbots Bromley (Staffordshire) still extant in the early nineteenth century.[106]

In the Datchworth tithing book a clutch of customary payments that appear near the end **[70]** are similar to *modi* but cannot be considered as such without knowing how long they had been in use. They were written out by Hawtayne's son when, one imagines, he was trying to make sense of the tithing system in the parish after the death of his father:

> To be paid in lieu of Tythe Milk & Calf for each Cow yearly   5s
> For Ewes in lieu of Tythe Lambs & Wool pr Score   10s
> For Weathers[107] Sheep in lieu of Wool & Herbage[108] pr Score 8s
> For each Tythe Pigg   2s

---

[103] HALS: DP78/3/2

[104] Tarver, *Church court records,* p103

[105] Tarver, *Church court records,* p103; Doree, *Thomas Hassall of Amwell,* p208

[106] E J Evans, *The contentious tithe,* (1976) p18

[107] wether or weather: a male sheep usually castrated and in its second season (Bristow, *Glossary,* p210)

[108] herbage: pertains to grazing

INTRODUCTION

These arrangements would have avoided all the complications of tithing milk, calves, lambs and fleeces in the manner described earlier.

Inflation over the years must have made some *modi* almost worthless but altering ancient agreements was very difficult. They were upheld if challenged in court providing they went back before 1189, and thus beyond the limit of legal memory, but by the end of the eighteenth century, it was deemed sufficient to accept the testimony of the oldest inhabitants, accompanied by evidence provided by receipts going back for a few generations.[109] If these conditions were not met, the parson had some hope of rescinding the old agreements.

Commutation of tithes also took the form of a composition agreement, made between the incumbent and a parishioner, that was to be paid annually in lieu of tithes in kind. The cautious incumbent would allow these agreements to run for a particular number of years, often three, and then review the amount. Others let the agreement remain for the lifetime of the payer and the collector, as long as the payer remained a parishioner. Edmund Lewin, rector of Westmill, made such agreements. For example, in 1731, William Clinton agreed to pay £9 15s 6d for tithes of his land 'as long as we shall both live in the parish'.[110]

Another case, in 1718, concerned Edward Brett of Thorley who paid rent of £24. An agreement was made between him and the parson, John Reynolds, that he should pay £3 per annum for his tithes 'for the future, as long as he holds the same land neither more nor less'. This was probably based on his rent and would have represented a rate of 2s 6d in the pound.[111] Reynolds also explained to his successors that Thorley had no 'modus's or customs of tithing' and the rector was at liberty to take all tithes in kind. However, 'as the Roads are bad for carrying off the Tith Corn, I advise my successors rather to compound than to take it in kind, … this one thing I only beg of them, not to accept of just the same summe for which I have compounded with them, lest they should in process of Time bring it into a modus'.

Although there are similarities between the two systems of commutation, the last example illustrates the clergy's dread of a *modus* with its long term

---

[109] Evans, *Contentious tithe*, pp19-20

[110] W A Pemberton, 'A parson's account book', *The Local Historian*, vol 3, 7, (1979), p399

[111] HALS: DP/108/3/2

commitment and permanent nature. The payers, on the other hand, must have tried hard to convince a new incumbent of the existence of such a method. A situation experienced and recorded in his tithing book by the new incumbent at Barnet, Richard Bundy, illustrates this point. Bundy arrived in 1731 to find a 'composition for Tythes in East Barnet' which he was told 'had stood upwards of forty years, and a pretended *modus* of twenty pence per Acre at High Barnet which they say has been for time immemorial, at least an hundred years'.[112] He felt that it was his duty to break through both these arrangements lest the church should suffer through his neglect. During his first year he persuaded some of the principal inhabitants to pay 2s in the pound rent at East Barnet and 2s per acre at High Barnet for a fixed period of three years. His final comment on the matter pointed out that, for the benefit of his successors, he would enter written agreements in the book, and, indeed, a number of agreements follow his account.

As vicar of Leighton Buzzard (Bedfordshire), Hawtayne was entitled to the small tithes although as an absentee vicar they were probably leased. These tithes are detailed in a glebe terrier, drawn up in 1709, that clearly illustrates customary payments in kind and *modi*.

> The Tythes due to the Vicar are as Followeth of Calves, Milk, Piggs, Geese, Eggs, Garden Fruits ... (vizt): for every barren Cow one penny halfpenny payable at Lamas; for every fruitful Cow twopence payable yearly at Lamas; for the Milk of every Calf under the number seven reared or brought up, one halfpenny at Lamas; for every calf under the number not reared but sold, the tenth part of the money for which tis sold but, if seven, eight, nine or ten happen to any one of the inhabitants in one year, one Calf of the seven, eight, nine or ten belongeth to the Vicar; for every henn two eggs yearly at Easter & three for a Cock. [113]

Glebe and glebe terriers

As already mentioned, during the period of prolific church building on large estates from the late seventh century, the lords of the manor often provided the resident priest with some land. This glebe land, as it was called, was a means of

---

[112] HALS: DP/16/3/1
[113] BLARS: CRT 170/2/15/2

providing for the priest's household and if large enough, could be a source of income. Once established, it continued to be part of the church benefice and was farmed by generations of incumbents. The glebe was often situated near the church or the parsonage but could also incorporate strips in the open fields. Glebe land was hardly ever sold and its position relative to surrounding strips remained unchanged despite informal enclosure that might be happening to adjacent strips in the open fields. Glebe land disappeared permanently if formal or parliamentary enclosures consolidated many strips, including the long established glebe. In this case, land was given in lieu of both the glebe and tithes to compensate the parson for the loss of his prime sources of income.[114]

The discussion about tithes above has noted the effects of inflation on long standing *modus* payments. During the sixteenth century this was a cause for concern among senior clergy. In order to monitor the financial situation of benefices, it was deemed necessary to submit a regular survey of each parish to the ecclesiastical authorities. Thus, in 1571, the glebe terrier evolved; in 1604 it was made a formal requirement, as stated in Canon 87.[115] A 'glebe terrier' was a list of all land and property belonging to the parish church, particularly details of the parsonage house and of the glebe land that could be farmed by the incumbent or leased to tenants. Although there was a demand for tithing customs to be included, this was met with mixed responses and it was not until 1698 that it became a definite requirement. Terriers, produced on average every five years, were inspected by the bishop and then kept in the bishop's or archdeacon's registry.[116] Parish copies were often made on odd pieces of paper or parchment, by their nature unlikely to survive; occasionally, a copy was made on some spare pages in the parish register.

A selection of Hertfordshire glebe terriers from the Archdeaconry of St Alban's (ASA), the Archdeaconry of Huntingdon, Hitchin Division (AHH) and parochial records has been investigated to establish the existence of tithe details before and after 1698, the date of obligation. Of the 22 from ASA that pre-dated 1698, 10 made a passing reference to tithes, such as Codicote (1637), 'Tythes due to

---

[114] Hey, *The Oxford Companion*, p204; S Hollowell, *Enclosure Records*, (Chichester, 2000), p20

[115] www.paleo.anglo-norman.org accessed 22 Aug 2008

[116] E J Evans, 'Tithing Customs and Disputes: the Evidence of Glebe Terriers, 1698-1850', *The Agricultural History Review,* 18.1 (1970), pp19-20; G H Tupling, 'Terriers and Tithe and Enclosure Awards', *The Amateur Historian*, vol 1, 12, (c1952-1955), p361

vicaridge Woole Lamb & Whittage[117]', and Bushey (1681), 'The tythes both great & small payable in kinde except Cowes. For the profit of each Cow is paid yearly fower pence in lieu of tythe by an ancient Custome.'[118] This collection of terriers contains only three that are dated after 1698 and none of these had the required addition of tithing customs.

Among the collection of parchment papers in AHH there is a handwritten transcription of some glebe terriers. The terriers from Watton-at-Stone dated 1638 and 1686 made no reference to tithes but that dated 1708 conformed to the 1698 requirement, and tithes of pigs, lambs, calves, milch cows and fleeces are given.[119]

Parish records reveal an example from Stevenage, where a 1706 glebe terrier contains a memorandum, added in 1778. This states that a carpenter, 'formerly Tithing Man', remembered that:

> The Custom of Tithing in the parish was, to take, first, the tenth shock of wheat, & then the eleventh alternately & like proportion for the odd shocks. The reason for taking it thus was in consideration of the Farmers Labour, in putting them into Shocks before they were tithed. He also says the custom was to take the tenth of all other things.[120]

The farmers and the tithe collector probably knew exactly what this meant.

A somewhat terser instruction is to be found in the 1815 terrier of Tewin: 'to the said Rectory belong all sorts of Tithe, both Great and small; there being no lands within the Parish exempt from Tithe, and no Prescriptions belonging to any particular farm, or parcel of ground'.[121] A Hitchin terrier, dated 1700, states that 'belonging to the vicarage of Hitchin …The Tythe of Wooll, & Lambes & Calves, & Milke & Pigeons & Fruite & Eggs & honey and Piggs'. Then, later, 'Ten pounds yearly to bee paid by the tenante of the great Tythe at

---

[117] whitage: the tithes of milk and butter (S Doree (ed), *The Parish Register and Tithing Book of Thomas Hassall of Amwell*, (Hertfordshire Record Society, 1989), p xxxix)
[118] HALS: ASA/3/1
[119] HALS: AHH/3/1
[120] HALS: DP/105/3/2, copy of a glebe terrier in a memorandum book kept by Rev Nicholas Cholwell
[121] 'No Prescriptions' probably meant that there were no customary payments; HALS: DP/106/1/2, parish register dated 1718-1812 with a copy of a terrier in the middle

each Lady Day & Michmas by Equall portions as by the Gift and order of the Master, Fellowes & Schollars of Trinity Colledge in Cambridge'.[122] The significance of this last item is provided by the earlier reference to 'the vicarage of Hitchin', quoted above. Trinity College, Cambridge was the rector at the time and thus had the right to the great tithes, but a customary agreement allowed the vicar to derive some benefit from them.

No Hertfordshire terrier has been found that matches the detail of tithes given in a 1707 terrier of Granborough (Buckinghamshire) or the 1709 Leighton Buzzard terrier, from which extracts about milk and calves have already been quoted.[123]

The Datchworth glebe

Although Hawtayne made several references to glebe land in his account book, there is no indication of its size. It is, however, possible to make an estimate by considering the 1607 glebe terrier and a survey made in 1829, (Figure 4).[124] The 1607 terrier follows the pattern required by the 1604 Canon. It describes the rectory with its surrounding buildings and also the glebe land, giving positions of the constituent parts near the rectory and in the open fields.[125] It estimates that 'lying about' the rectory were ten acres of land 'more or lesse'. In the open fields there were said to be about six acres in Cundell Field and four acres in Chibden Field, so in total there were some 20 acres. The survey of 1829 recorded a total of almost 24 acres consisting of about 14 acres adjacent to the rectory, of which nearly half were arable, and just over nine acres in the open fields. The 'more or lesse' aspect of measuring acreages in the seventeenth century may account for the difference between the two totals. Whatever the explanation, Hawtayne had somewhere between 20 and 24 acres of glebe during his incumbency. The reason for the 1829 survey is unclear but it serves as a useful snapshot of the open fields as they were then, about 100 years after Hawtayne's time. The whole parish is represented in Figure 1; Figure 4 shows an enlargement of the northern section in which the open fields were spread out. The stippled parts indicate the positions of the glebe strips. The question arises as to whether these strips were those described in the 1607 terrier and thus were

---

[122] HALS: DP/53/1/3, parish register dated 1679-1746/7 with a terrier at the end
[123] see pp xxxiii, xxxvi
[124] HALS: DP/33/29/2
[125] See Appendix 1 for complete transcription; HALS: DP/33/1/1

the ones farmed by Hawtayne in the early eighteenth century. The two surveys have been compared from this point of view.

In the 200 years or so separating the two surveys, the names of the principle 'common' fields have changed. Clues from the orientation of the strips in 'Cundell Field' described in 1607 suggest that this field was to the west of the road leading to Bragbury End, and in 1829 was mainly called 'Sliding Dale Common'.

An extract from the 1607 terrier describes the positions of four of the strips in relation to this lane which have been represented diagrammatically in Figure 5.

> **Item** there belonge unto the sayd rectorie 6 acres of arable land more or lesse, lying in a common feild there called Cundell whearof one acre and a halfe more or less lyeth betweene the lands of George Shotboult South & the lands of Thomas Kimpton North & abutteth uppon the lane wich leadeth from Brackburie ende to Thatchworth Church East, & the lands of Richard Kimpton West. [126]
>
> And one other part in the sayd feild, contayning one acre more or less lyeth betweene the lands of Thomas Kimpton South and the lands of Thomas Foster North: and abutteth uppon the forsayde lane leading from Brackburie End to Thatchworth Church East, & the lands of Thomas Foster West.
>
> And one other part in the forsayd common feild contayning one acre & halfe more or less lyeth between the forenamed lane which leadeth from Brackburie End to Thatchworth Church East & the lands of Richard Rudd on the West & abutteth uppon sayd lane north & uppon the land of Francis Bigg South.
>
> And one other part in the forsayd common feild contayning by estimation one acre more or less lyeth between the lands of Thomas Foster West and the lands of William Rudd East, & abutteth uppon the land of John Man North & of Francis Bigg South'.

The position of this group in relation to the lane has enabled it to be identified as the group that includes the strip called Little Oak Tree Common in 1829 (Figure

---

[126] Brackburie End is Bragbury End; Thatchworth was another name for Datchworth

4). This satisfactory match provides a persuasive argument that the other 'acres' described in 1607 were represented by the rest of the stippled strips shown in Figure 4.[127]

That 'Cundell Field' in 1607 was Sliding Dale Common in 1829 is confirmed in a document relating to a land conveyance in 1853 that referred to 'a Common Field called Cundell and now Slidingdale Common'.[128] Similarly, Chibden Field, referred to later in the 1607 terrier, was substantially renamed Datchworth Common. Confirmation of this is provided by some title deeds of *c*1818 revealing that 'Church Field ... containing by estimation 3a, 1r, 8p' was formerly called Chipden or Childen.[129] This field, containing 3a, 1r, 7p in 1839, is visible in Figure 3, where it was then part of Datchworth Common. Brief references by Hawtayne in his lists of landholdings reveal that the open fields were still called Cundell Common **[10]** and Chibden Common **[13]** during his incumbency. Having established that the glebe lands remained unchanged from 1607 to 1829, it is safe to assume that these were the lands farmed or leased by Hawtayne in the early 1700s.

---

[127] See Appendix 1
[128] HALS: DE/AS/1435
[129] HALS: DE/AS/1595; a = acres, r = roods, p = poles

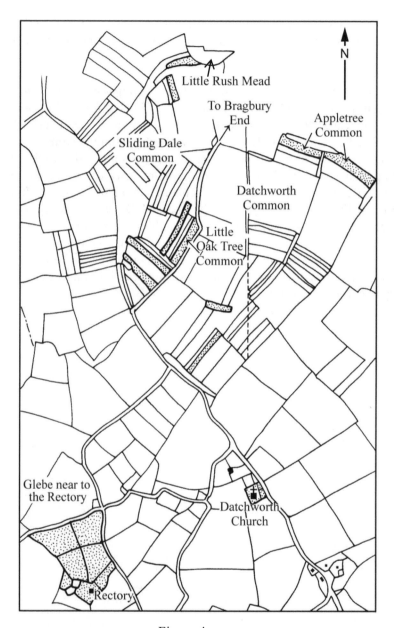

Figure 4
The glebe (stippled area) in 1829 was nearly 24 acres: 9 acres in the open
fields and 14½ acres near the rectory and round the church

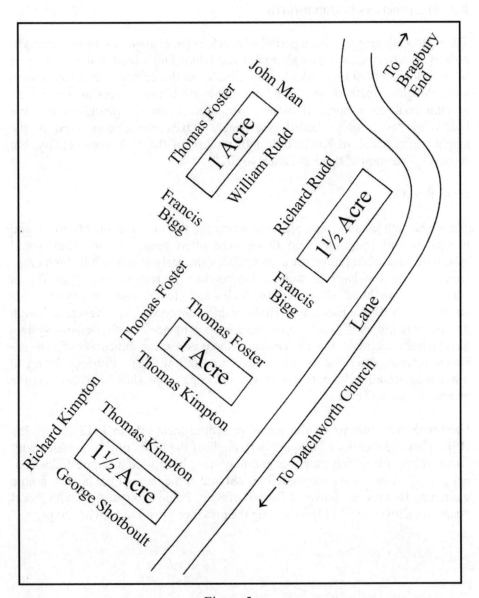

Figure 5
Interpretation of the 1607 terrier description of Glebe land in Cundell Field
and its position in relation to the lane between Datchworth Church and
Bragbury End.

INTRODUCTION

Farming practices in Datchworth

The eighteenth century was a period of accelerating change in farming methods, notably improvements in plough design and Jethro Tull's seed drill, but many of the developments did not take hold until later in the century. It is not known what ploughing methods were used in Datchworth but references in Hawtayne's account book to 'a horse at Plowe' [8] suggests that the plough in use was lightweight as it only needed one beast. Oxen were being used in the neighbouring parish of Knebworth until the end of the eighteenth century, but there is no mention of these in Datchworth.[130]

Crop Rotation

The eighteenth century was also important for the introduction of clover and turnips as soil improvers and these were often sown on land that would otherwise have been fallow for a year. From the early to mid-1700s both crops were used in the Norfolk four-course rotation system so that, typically, a combination might be wheat, turnips, barley and clover. Soon this system was adopted by Suffolk, Essex and Hertfordshire farmers.[131] However, although turnips were grown in Datchworth, there is no evidence of a four-course system having been adopted. On the contrary, there is a clear indication of a three-course rotation described as 'tilt', 'edge' and fallow [10]. Entries relating to tithes paid according to acreages of tilt and edge crops show that this was the accepted system (Table 1).

Hawtayne grew turnips on the glebe, recording their sale in 1712 for £3 15s [15]. They are mentioned frequently throughout the book, often combined with 'small tithes' for tithing purposes and may have been used as cattle fodder but not grazed. Vetches are mentioned [5, 28] and at the back of the book is a note written by Hawtayne: 'Sowed 4 Bushill of Saint Foine upon an Acre with 3 or 4 pounds of Clover seed' [74] indicating the presence of soil improving crops.

---

[130] F A Richardson, *Knebworth, the story of a Hertfordshire village*, (Hertford, 1982), p39
[131] Hey, *The Oxford Companion*, p454

(1) Page number	(2) Year	(3) Name	(4) Tilt	(5) Edge	(6) Actual Tithe			(7) Expected tithe		
			Acres	Acres	£	s	d	£	s	d
[30]	1716	E Mardell	-	3	0	6	0	0	6	0
[30]	1716	W Butterfield	15	20	5	0	0	5	0	0
[30]	1716	W Kimpton	8	32½	**5**	**9**	**0**	4	17	0
[30]	1716	J Whitfield	8	9	**3**	**0**	**0**	2	10	0
[30]	1716	J Blindall	2	1	0	10	0	0	10	0
[30]	1716	W Pennyfather	20	-	**1**	**17**	**0**	4	0	0
[32]	1717	Mr Eyres	3	-	0	12	0	0	12	0
[32]	1717	T Freeman	4	5	**1**	**1**	**0**	1	6	0
[37]	1719	T Adams	16½	-	3	6	0	3	6	0
[38]	1720	J Mardell	½	-	0	2	0	0	2	0

Table 1: Occurrences of tilt and edge crops. (Column 7, 'Expected tithe' has been calculated using tilt at 4s per acre and edge at 2s per acre.)

Tilth, or as Hawtayne recorded it, 'tilt', literally means cultivated soil, but it had a more specific meaning when used as part of crop rotation. It referred to the land that had been fallow, then ploughed ready for the winter sowing of wheat or rye. After the harvest, in the winter of the following year, the wheat stubble would be ploughed in ready for the spring sowing of barley, oats, peas or beans. This was called etch crop as it was sown on ground from which a crop had been taken.[132] Datchworth and Walkern referred to it as 'edge' crop whereas Barley used 'each' and Clothall, 'eddish'.

Generally, Hawtayne calculated his tithes using rates of 4s per acre for tilt and 2s per acre for edge. A comparison between columns 6 and 7 (Table 1) reveals some inconsistencies (in bold type). The discrepancies are not remarkable except for W Pennyfather's entry where the actual tithe suggests that a different valuation may have been used or possibly one of the entries was inaccurate. It is of interest to compare Datchworth's annual rates per acre with those in other Hertfordshire parishes where records survive (Table 2).[133]

---

[132] etch: a corruption of 'eddish'; stubble that was broken up and ploughed for spring sowing. (*OED* and S Coleman and J Wood, *Historic landscape and archaeology glossary of terms,* (Bedfordshire, 1985), p55)
[133] HALS: DP/8/3/1; DP/13/3/3; DP/114/3/7; DP/30/3/2; DP/120/3/4

Parish	Year	Tilth (per acre)	Etch(per acre)
Aspenden	1722	5s	-
Barley	1732	3s	2s
Barley	1773	4s	2s 9d
Clothall	1747	6s	-
Datchworth	1716	4s	2s
Walkern	1743/4	5s	2s 6d
Westmill	1685	5s	2s 6d

Table 2: Tithe rates for tilth and etch crops in other Hertfordshire parishes.

Tilth crop was more highly valued than the etch crop and was tithed at roughly twice the latter's rate (Table 2). Though small, the sample gives an indication of variations between parishes and shows, in the case of Barley, that a difference of forty years had made only a small difference to the rates.

The Crops

In the Datchworth tithe accounts, specific crops were occasionally mentioned such as oats, vetches, peas and rye; of these four examples, rye was the tilth crop at 4s per acre as the tithe paid indicated [35]. Other crops, mainly wheat and barley, are revealed in Hawtayne's record of corn sales, usually at Hertford market, from 1711 until 1717 ([5-7], [15-16], [18], [29], [31], [33]). Average crop prices in shillings per quarter obtained by the rector (Haw) have been compared with averages for the Home Counties (HC) from 1710 to 1719 in Table 3.[134] Most of Hawtayne's averages compare favourably with the Home Counties averages, only the pea crop is significantly below the Home Counties ten year average.

Barley		Oats		Rye		Wheat		Peas	
Haw	HC	Haw	HC	Haw	HC	Haw	HC	Haw	HC
18.93	21.46	13.98	13.81	26.18	25.03	37.43	37.81	20.31	30.70

Table 3: Prices in shillings per quarter for Hawtayne's sales compared with Home Counties averages calculated for 1710-1719

[134] P J Bowden, 'Statistics', in J Thirsk, (ed), *The Agrarian History of England and Wales*, vol V, 1640-1750, (Cambridge, 1985), pp864-869

The quantities of crops sold have been summarised in Figure 6.[135] There is no record for 1714.

Income from crops and tithes

Figure 6 needs some explanation. First, in 1711 and 1712 the corn sold would have probably been a combination of tithes taken in kind and produce from the glebe. Secondly, details of crop acreage and crop yield are unavailable so a reasoned explanation for the difference in grain produce between 1711 and 1712 cannot be made. Even without such information 1712 appears to be a poor year in comparison with 1711. Thirdly, composition agreements made in 1712 **[9]** have become manifest in 1713 thus reducing tithes taken in kind and the sale thereof. Figure 7 illustrates the transition years of 1711 to 1717 when, from 1713, composition payments became a prominent feature in Hawtayne's tithe collection. It also serves as an indication of his income for the first seven years of his incumbency.

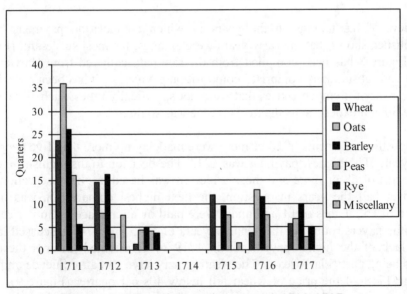

Figure 6: Sales of crops (in quarters) 1711-1717

---

[135] miscellany: a mixture of wheat and rye that provided flour for bread called 'maslin' (Ernle, *English farming past and present,* p8)

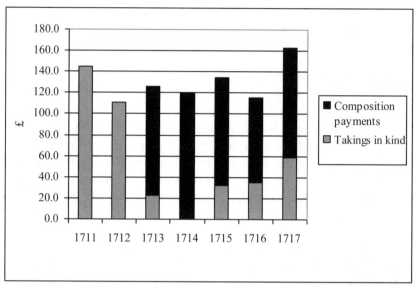

Figure 7: Tithes taken in kind and as compositions 1711-1717

A view of his takings in the years in which composition payments were established shows that the early years were amongst his most successful (Figure 8). Figure 8 has been compiled from the raw data gathered from Hawtayne's book and substantially comprises composition payments. It has been considered unnecessary to remove entries that were not specifically tithes, such as rent and some funeral expenses, as their occurrence was so rare.

Composition payments of £8 or more were made by no more than five people in any year. The highest payment was £21. The decision to distinguish between payments of £8 or more and those under £8 was based on the observation that for over half the years in question, the next highest composition was in the region of £5. Tithes of £1 and under were paid by an average of 36 per cent of the tithe payers (omitting the peculiar years of 1745 and 1747 discussed later). The lack of the higher payers during 1719-24 contributed towards these six years being particularly lean. The weather may have had an influence and also during 1718-24 the price of wheat fell below 40s per quarter (Figure 9). One could almost conclude that higher composition payers responded to the poor value of wheat by deciding not to renew their agreements. There appears to have been a similar response in the interval 1737-39. Two tenants, Thomas Kimpton of Swangleys and James Whitehall of Datchworthbury, may have responded in this way.[136] However, the other two troughs (1730-1734 and 1742-1747) (Figure 9) do not seem to have had a marked effect on the higher payers' contributions, thus suggesting that the fall in the price of wheat does not tell the full story. It is worth investigating the five tithe payers who stopped paying high compositions before 1719.

William Wallis agreed a composition of £8 10s in 1713 **[21]** which he paid regularly, although on one occasion in 1714, he paid 'with a bad Crown Piece' **[24]**. As Hawtayne put a line through this comment the matter must have been resolved. Wallis left Datchworth in 1719.

John Flindall of Swangleys Farm, agreed a composition of £9 10s in 1712 **[9]** but died shortly after in 1713.[137] His son, Robert Flindall, agreed the same amount **[26]**, which he paid in 1715, then no more. The family left the farm at the end of the lease in 1723.[138]

William Blindall in 1712 agreed a composition of £11 10s **[9]**, and again in 1715 **[27]**. From 1718 to 1721, he paid small tithes. From 1725 payments of £11 are apparent **[43]**. He died in 1734, aged 85.[139]

Thomas Goose agreed to pay £20 per year in 1713 **[20]**, continuing with this amount until 1718. He then paid small tithes until he died in 1721, aged 76.

John Tompson agreed to pay £16 in 1712 **[9]**. He managed £15 in 1713 and £10 in 1714. There are no subsequent entries. His burial cannot be found in Datchworth records so he may have moved away.

The combined effect of the various family circumstances noted above contributed towards the reduced receipts for the years 1719-24 that were particularly poor for William Hawtayne. In later years it is possible to observe other higher payers emerging, for example James Whitehall of Datchworthbury, Thomas Kimpton of Swangleys Farm, William Game of Raffin Green Farm and John Crawley of Bragbury End Farm.

---

[136] See Appendix 2 'Landowners and Tenants'
[137] HALS: DP/62/1/3.
[138] The Workers Educational Association, *Knebworth, the story of our village*, (Knebworth, 1967) p13
[139] HALS: DP/33/1/2; Hawtayne often included ages in the burial register

INTRODUCTION

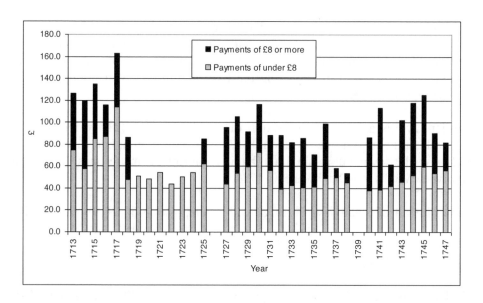

Figure 8: Income from tithes and the glebe 1713-1747

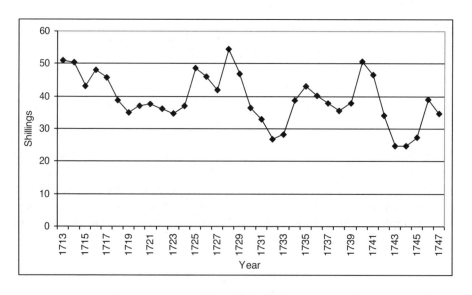

Figure 9: The price of wheat 1713-1747[140]

---

[140] J M Stratton, *Agricultural records AD220-1977* (R Whitlock (ed.), 2nd edition, 1978), pp68-76

INTRODUCTION

Hawtayne's expenses and taxes

Hawtayne's records of his own expenses are sparse. He gives lists of disbursements in the years 1711-13 (**[4]**, **[8]**, **[17]**, **[19]**), then a note of expenses in 1717 of £51 5s 3d but with no details. There is no other mention of his outgoings. It is possible to learn something of his other financial commitments by consulting Datchworth churchwardens' accounts and land tax returns. The clergy paid tax on glebe land and tithes, which caused Hawtayne to be one of the highest tax payers in the parish.[141] In 1721, his land tax payment of £13 10s was second only to Mr Miles, the tenant of Datchworthbury (Appendix 4). Based on the rate for 1721, which was 3s in the pound, the valuation of Hawtayne's glebe and tithes was £90.[142] In the same year assessments were made for poor relief at a rate of 6d in the pound. Hawtayne's dues of £2 5s confirm his glebe and tithe valuation at £90 (Appendix 5). His valuation of £90 in the land tax returns remained consistent for subsequent years but the poor relief lists for 1731 and 1744 appear to have been based on a valuation of £50 for his glebe and tithes.[143] The assessor for the payment of poor relief was usually the overseer, whose decision was subject to the agreement of the vestry.[144] Land tax had three assessors who were usually the collectors as well. In 1731 they were John Field, John Godfrey and John Goose, all of whose names appear in churchwardens' accounts and so would have been at vestry meetings. It can only be assumed that this concession in Hawtayne's valuation for poor relief was agreed by the vestry.

Value of the glebe and tithes and annual takings

It is appropriate to sum up Hawtayne's takings by comparing them against the assessed value of his glebe and tithes. In 1709, when Hawtayne was inducted at Datchworth, the glebe and tithes were leased to Richard Pilgrim for £116 **[2]** by the previous incumbent, John Gaile. At the beginning of the tenancy thirteen years previously, his rent had been £130, it was later reduced to £124 and finally to £116.

---

[141] H G Hunt, 'Land tax assessments', in K M Thompson, (ed), *Short guides to records* (The Historical Association, 1994), p87; funds from taxation of 'every inhabitant, parson, vicar', Poor Law 1601, (W E Tate, *The Parish Chest* (Cambridge, 1969) p191
[142] HALS: Land Tax, Datchworth
[143] HALS: DP/33/8/1
[144] Tate, *Parish Chest*, p29

INTRODUCTION

Table 4 summarises Pilgrim's valuations together with estimates calculated from land tax returns from 1715.

Year	Leased	The Hawtayne years						
	Pre-1711	1711-1714	1715	1716	1718	1719	1720	1721-1747
Rent valuation	£130, £124, £116	Not known	£108	£108	£103	£100	£100	£90

Table 4: Datchworth tithe and glebe valuation

The average of Hawtayne's takings from 1711 to 1720 was £117 2s 0d which was just above the valuation of £116 in 1711 when he 'took the Tythes into [his] Own Hands'[2]. There are no land tax records from 1711 to 1714 so the valuation is not known. The downward trend in valuation is plain to see until 1721, after which it remained at £90 for the rest of Hawtayne's incumbency. This appears to have been a realistic amount when compared with his average takings of £80 15s 10d from 1721 to1747.

Hawtayne's income from Elstree in the years 1709 to 1718 is unknown. The glebe at Elstree consisted of two acres in 1650 and was probably the same size in Hawtayne's time, small but nevertheless valued at £40.[145] It may not have been sufficient for his needs when he lived at Elstree because there are references about supplies, such as wheat, peas, oats and barley, being sent there from Datchworth between 1711 and 1715, ([5-7], [15], [18], [29]). By the time Hawtayne's grandson was rector at Elstree in 1787, the common had been enclosed (1776) and about 200 acres of land given to the rectory in lieu of tithes.[146] No record of tithe collection at Elstree has been found.

As vicar of Shephall (1718-33) Hawtayne was entitled to small tithes, and, unusually, the great tithes as well, as observed earlier. Later (1733-47), he could have received small tithes from Leighton Buzzard (1733-47), but as an absentee vicar this may have been impractical.

---

[145] D Lysons, *The Environs of London, Volume the Fourth, Counties of Herts, Essex & Kent*, ((1796), pp26-27
[146] HALS: DP/36/3/1

INTRODUCTION

Tithe takings in 1745 and 1747

Apart from 1745 and 1747, the average number of tithe payers per year was about 30, ranging from 26 to 43. Very few paid under two shillings. In 1745 and 1747, 77 and 75 payers were listed respectively of which 23 and 24 paid less than two shillings. In both years the list of payers was more than twice as long as the average for any other year and there was a marked increase in the number of people who paid low amounts. It may be no coincidence that this change of habit occurred near the end of Hawtayne's life when he may have been receiving assistance from his son who was possibly the scribe that contributed a few of the early entries for 1745 **[63]**. The 1746 record was completed by Hawtayne but on the next page was a Memorandum, in his son's hand, relating to some standard tithe payments such as lambs and turnips **[66]**. Many of the 1747 entries were written by Hawtayne's son.

Estimates of land values

Some acreages were recorded by Hawtayne near the start of the tithing book (**[10]** to **[14]**). Table 5 has been compiled using these entries and rental values from the 1715 land tax return for Datchworth.

Landlord	Tenant	Acres	Rental values 1715	Per acre
Mr Hawkings **[10]**	John Whitfield	50.75	£26	10s 3d
Mr Audley **[11]**	John Ipgrave	30	£14	9s 4d
Joseph Caughton **[11]**	Michael Ireland	12	£5	8s 4d
Mrs Knight **[12]**	William Butterfield	50	£23	9s 2d
William Dardes **[13]**	-	45	£10	4s 5d
Esquire Lytton **[13]**	William Emmins	85	£24	5s 8d
Rowland Mardell **[13]**	-	41.5	£25	12s 1d
Robert King **[14]**	William Kimpton	44	£18	8s 2d

Table 5: Land valuation based on acreages and 1715 land tax rental values

Variation in the value of land is to be expected according to the proportion of arable to pasture, and perhaps woodland. The average, based on the figures above, is about 8s 1d. This figure should be treated with caution as it is unclear whether land tax was necessarily paid on the acreages quoted in Table 5. Tenancies could be fluid.

INTRODUCTION

A valuation can also be calculated by using the acreage of the parish quoted by *The Victoria County History* in 1908. It was then stated that of a total of 2,018 acres about 1,500 acres were arable, the rest being mostly grass with 18 acres of woodland. Using the first figure and the total parish rental value in 1715, (£813), the average value is about 8s 1d. Similar calculations made for Elstree and Shephall produce land value estimates of 10s 2d and 9s 2d respectively.[147] A comparison has been made with some land values in Cheshire dated *c*1744-49.[148] Nearly 8,500 acres were involved in the analysis and the value ranged from 9s per acre to 14s per acre with an average of 11s per acre. It is not altogether clear whether the land was exclusively arable. Despite the geographical disparity of the two regions, and the gap of 30 years or so between the two studies, the land values are remarkably similar.

People in the parish

Curates

The earliest mention of a curate is in some vestry notes dated 1710, when the churchwardens' accounts were signed by William Dechair, curate.[149] He was appointed in 1709.[150] The next reference is in 1712, when a curate named Rev Mr Thomas Hind left the parish following the death of his wife 'in Child Bed of the small pox' on the day after the baptism and burial of their daughter.[151] An entry was made in the burial register in 1713 stating that several burials had not been recorded 'by the neglect of Mr Waller'. Judging by the handwriting, someone other than Hawtayne had added the names of the people concerned: probably both Mr Waller and the unknown scribe were curates. The curate about whom there is most evidence is Mr Betham, who was in charge from December 1714 until April 1718. There is a page in Hawtayne's account book [73] that is devoted to financial transactions between him and the rector. Other curates appointed during Hawtayne's incumbency were Robert James (1733 and 1734) and John Rawbone (1741),[152] neither of whom appears in the tithing account book.

---

[147] HALS: Land Tax, Datchworth; W Page (ed), *VCH Hertfordshire,* vol II, pp349, 443
[148] C F Foster, *Four Cheshire townships in the 18th century, Arley, Appleton, Stockton Heath and Great Budworth* (Cheshire, 1992) p12
[149] HALS: DP/33/8/1
[150] CCED, accessed 2 March 2009
[151] HALS: DP/33/1/2
[152] CCED

INTRODUCTION

Parish officials

Churchwardens
In the accounts, the names are not always given, but between 1709 and 1746 the following parishioners held office: John Bassett, senior and junior, Thomas Goose, William Wallis, James Whitehall, William Game and Richard Blindall.

Overseers of the poor
Names were entered more regularly for this office and included the following, (in chronological order and avoiding repeats): Thomas Coulson, Daniel Crawley, William Blindall, Rowland Mardell, John Whitfield, William Butterfield, John Godfrey, Robert Heath, William Kimpton, William Whittenborough, James Whitehall, John Phipp, John Bassett, John Goose, John Field, Joseph Hudson, William Wallis, William Blindall (another), Richard Blindall, John Whittenbery, John Crawley, Thomas Neats and Benjamin Whittenbury

Constables
A few intermittent entries were made in the early years and then in the 1730s as follows: John Bassett junior, John Whitfield (for three consecutive years), Rowland Mardell and Edward Gray (two consecutive years).

Stone Wardens[153]
There were only two entries for this position: 1711, Thomas Kimpton and Daniel Mardell and 1712, Thomas Kimpton and John Flindall. In 1735, John Goose and John Smith were listed as surveyors.

Land and Window tax assessors and collectors
The assessors and the collectors were very often the same for land tax as for window tax. Taking 1715 as an example, the assessors for window tax were William Blindall, John Whitfield and Mr Goose and the associated collectors were Daniel Crawley and William Wallis. These men took the same responsibility for land tax apart from Mr Goose.

---

[153] stone wardens, also called surveyors of the highways, were responsible for the maintenance of roads

INTRODUCTION

Protestant Dissenters

As a postscript to this section on parish officials, it is appropriate to mention that of the officers above, Edward Gray, Thomas Coulson, John Bassett and William Kimpton are on a list of Protestant dissenters, dated 13 October 1719, who expressed their intention to meet for religious worship at 'a place called Petits'.[154] Presumably this announcement was obligatory as part of the Toleration Act of 1689, when congregations of Protestant non-conformists were allowed to worship providing that their meeting house was licensed at quarter sessions.[155] That dissenters held positions as parish officials is not altogether a surprise when set beside examples in London of Quakers who, though they refused to pay tithes and poor relief, nevertheless held parochial office after 1689.[156]

Last words

There was no particular format for recording tithe payment, each rector or vicar had his own method, either inherited or developed to his satisfaction. This is evident when browsing through available records. In the cases of Westmill and Aspenden, farms were listed with associated landowners and tenants, sometimes with a table of contents at the front of the book referring to numbered pages. Sufficient space was allotted to account for tithes over several years.[157] In the early part of a Walkern tithe book, for each year, there were lists of names in no particular order. About a quarter of the names in 1740 had no amounts recorded signifying no tithe payment. Later in the book, the names were in alphabetical order.[158] In a tithe book for Barley, every detail of each person's tithe was listed, recording tithes on crops, cows, sheep, etc, providing a rather messy presentation but packed with information.[159] Hawtayne's method gives a year by year picture of his collecting but rarely records names of defaulters. The omission of payers of lower calibre tithes until the last year or two of the book is

---

[154] W Urwick, *Non conformity in Hertfordshire being lectures upon the nonconforming worthies of St Albans and memorials of Puritanism and Nonconformity in all the parishes of the county of Hertford*, (1884) p576

[155] Hey, *The Oxford companion*, p441

[156] S Dixon, 'Quakers and the London parish 1670-1720', *The London Journal*, vol 32, no 3, (Nov 2007), p239

[157] HALS: DP/120/3/4; HALS: DP/8/3/1

[158] HALS: DP/114/3/7

[159] HALS: DP/14/3/3

INTRODUCTION

a subject of curiosity. It remains, nevertheless, a remarkable record over a period of nearly 37 years.

The Book

The Reverend William Hawtayne kept tithe and glebe accounts of Datchworth almost continuously from 1711 to 1747. The record is substantially that of his collection of tithes throughout the period, together with early references to his farming of the glebe. In the first few years there were pages devoted to financial transactions relating to the marketing of crops and other produce, some from the glebe and others were tithes taken in kind. He made purchases too and the related disbursements were also meticulously listed.

The book itself is roughly A4 in size, covered in fawn vellum, with some faded, illegible writing on the front and back covers. The pages are ruled to accommodate £ s d and are not numbered. For ease of reference in the text and the Introduction, the pages of the document have been assigned notional numbers. The first page of importance is page **[2]** that contains Hawtayne's notes about his induction. This page is preceded by two pages, one badly torn and illegible, and the second, numbered **[1]**, contains a list of payments unrelated to any other transactions and has been included with other miscellaneous notes at the end of the transcription. The information on **[8]** has been entered out of order by the rector. To maintain a logical sequence, it has been placed after **[4]**.

There are several instances of different people with identical names appearing in the text. Appendices 2 (Noteworthy landowners and tenants) and 3 (Burials and wills of Datchworth tithe payers found between 1711 and 1747) may help unravel apparent ambiguities.

The final tithe entries in 1747 are followed by some empty pages and then there are some miscellaneous notes and accounts at the back. These latter pages have been numbered by the editor as though they followed on directly without the intervening empty pages.

DATCHWORTH TITHE ACCOUNTS

1711-1747

TITHE ACCOUNTS

[2] *The induction of the Reverend William Hawtayne to Datchworth 1709*[1]

I was inducted into the Rectory of Datchworth in the ~~Year~~ 27th Day of November in the year 1709 it being of a Sunday.

I found the Glebe Land and all the Tythes both great & small Let to a Tennant (Richard Pilgrim) for three years by Lease at one Hundred an twenty four pounds per Annum but in consideration of some Losses that he had received by his Under Tennants Mr John Gale[2] my Predecessor had made him an abatement of Eight pounds yearly for these three last years ~~so that the Rent~~ now by a note under his hand. So that tho' the Lease was for £124 yearly as above yet the Rent to be pd was only an £116. Which accordingly I receive of Richard Pilgrim whose Term of three years expired at Midsummer 1711. At which time I took the Tythes into my Own Hands An Account of which follows on the other side.[3]

Richard Pilgrim rented the Rectory (nothing but surplice Fees & halfe the Parsonage House reserved) thirteen years at these Severall Rates he pd at first as I am told an £130 yearly for it then an £124 for 6 or 9 years and then for 3 years at £116.

For the Quiet of the Parishioners to whom Pilgrim had let most of their Tythes severally I confirm Mr Gales agreement with him for those three years running at his Death. Tho' I was not obliged to do it by Law.

[3] An Account of what I have laid out at Datchworth in Ending of the Great Tythes of the Whole Parish in the Year 1711

Three Tything Men Hired for the Whole Harvest {	Kemp	02	15 00
	William Hoare	02	12 06
	Edward Webster	02	12 06
Edward Williams a Labourer		02	12 06
Jeakes himselfe his Son three Horses and two Carts for the whole Harvest		06	00 00
Thomas Naysh and his Son		03	10 00
Hired one Horse & Cart more		01	[*blank*]
Gave all these People Gloves at one shilling a pare which with my own Servants		00	08 00

---

[1] **[1]** is among the miscellaneous items at the end, after **[74]**
[2] See Introduction: n30
[3] See **[3].**

1

		£ sh d
Besides these I had one Servant of my own and two Horses and a Cart		04 00 00
This with what I gave in Largesse as under written was what it cost me in the whole for I found the men with no diet[4] but a Harvest home dinner for which I charge		00 15 00

Gave in Largesse

	£ sh d
To Adams's men at Welshes	00 00 06
To the men at the Berry	00 05 00
To Mr Randall's men at the Bridge Foot	00 01 06
To Mr Pennyfather's men	00 01 00
To Mr Emmans's men	00 02 00
To Mr King's men	00 03 00
To Wallis's men	00 02 00
To Mr Goose's men	00 02 06
Daniell Crawley's men	00 01 00
William Whittenborough's men	00 01 00
Flindall's men	00 03 00
Blindall's men	00 03 06
Whitfield's & North's men 2 shillings Each	00 04 00
Largesse total	01 10 00

[4] An Account of my Disbursements at Datchworth 1711

2d [2nd][5]

		£ sh d
	Pd Goodman Williams for Thrashing of Rye	00 08 00
Jul 28	Charges at Hartford when I sold two Loads	00 01 00
	For a Fan to dress Corn with	00 04 00
	For 5 sieves	00 04 06
	For one sieve more a Large one	00 01 06
	For two Sacks	00 06 00
	For five Sacks more	00 12 00

---

[4] 'no diet' meant that food was not given as part payment for farm labourers' work.
[5] The label '2d' by Hawtayne links [4] with [8] where disbursements for 1711 are continued. [8] has been placed after [4] to maintain continuity.

	For a Bushill & Shovell for the Barn[6]	00	05	00
	For a Shovell & Curry Comb & Mane Comb	00	03	00
	For a Cutting Knife in the Barn	00	03	06
	~~Pd Williams and Titmasse \for/ of thrashing of Rye~~	~~00~~	~~0~~	
Sep 1	Charges at Hartford	00	01	09
Sep 8	Charges at Hartford	00	02	01½
8	Pd ~~those~~ \one/ man for Thrashing 35 days with Bear	01	17	06
Sep 22	Charges at Hartford	00	01	04
29	Charges at Hartford	00	04	10
Oct 20	Charges at Hartford	00	01	06
	Laid out for a Riddle for Pease	00	01	04
	For a Lantern	00	01	04
	For 2 Plowes and two Harrows	02	10	00
	For mending one Plowe	00	02	06
Oct 22	Charges at Hartford when sold 3 Quarter of Barley	00	01	08
Oct 27	Charges at Hartford	00	01	10
	Locks[7] & Halters	00	02	02
	Pd Titmasse for Thrashing & 3 days Sowing	01	09	00
	Pd Tyler for Thrashing 34 days	01	14	00
	For both their bear for those days at 2d	00	11	00
	Pd them both for Wood Work 11 days & ½	01	03	00
	For their bear those 11 days & ½ at 2d a day	00	03	10
	Pd Titmasse for a Flail	00	00	06
Nov 3	Charges at Hartford	00	01	06
	Pd Williams for Thrashing 3sh[8] then due to him	00	12	00
Nov 17	Pd Williams for Thrashing twelve shillings	00	12	00
	[*Total*]	[*14*	*5*	*10½*]

---

[6] A bushel is a measuring device that holds four pecks.
[7] 'Lock' probably referred to a chain and metal clasp that could be attached to a halter.
[8] 3 shillings is not consistent with the amount entered.

[8] An Account of my Disbursements at Datchworth 1711

From page 2d [9]

Nov 17	Charges at Hartford when sold ten Quarter of Barley	00	01	02
	For bottoming of chaffe sieve	00	00	06
	For two Piggs bought at Hartford	00	14	00
Dec 16	Charges at Hartford when I sold 8 Loads of Wheat			
	For sack carrying & other expenses at Markett	00	02	08
	For Francis Board ten days at Datchworth	00	06	04
	Paid to Jeakes for going to Plowe	00	06	00
	For a horse to go to Plowe 7 days, 2 keeping	00	07	00
	For a pound of Candles & some salt	00	00	08
	For a pound of Grease for cart wheels	00	00	03½
Dec 23	Charges at Hartford when sold 2 Loads of wheat	00	02	09
	Paid more to Williams for Thrashing	00	[blank]	
[1711/12] Jan 17	Charges at Hartford when sold 5 Quarter & ½ of Barley	00	01	00
	For half a pound of Candles & Franciss Board	00	10	00
	For Thomas's Board there	00	03	00
Feb 9	Charges at Hartford when sold 6 Quarter of Oates	00	02	07
Feb 23	Charges at Hartford when sold 6 Quarter 2 B[ushel] of Oates	00	01	08
	For a horse at Plowe 6 days	00	06	00
	For cutting 45 Bushill of Chaffe	00	03	09
	To James for my Board	00	10	00
Mar 29	For Francis for 19 days Board at Datchworth	00	10	08
	For a fortnights Board for Francis more	00	08	07
	For whip cord & Grease	00	00	03
Apr	For bear[10] when the Heiffers came home	00	01	00
	Paid to Jeakes for spreading of Dung	00	02	06
	For the hire of his Mare 7 days	00	03	06

---

[9] See note to [4].
[10] bear: beer

For his Boy 7 days at Plow	00	03	06
For thrashing of Pease & Beans	00	01	00
Pd to Harding[11] for cutting of 39 Bushills of Chaffe	00	03	03

[Total] *[5 13 7½]*

[5] An Account of What I have sold at Datchworth of Corn and Strawe

Sep 1711		£	sh	d
Jul 28	Sold at Hartford 2 Horse Loads of Rye	01	18	00
idem[12]	Sold one load more at Home	00	19	00
Aug 3	Sold one load more at Home	00	19	10
24	Sold two load more at Home	01	16	00
Sep 8	Sold one load more of Rye at Home	00	16	00
	Sowed myself nine bushills of Rye[13]	01	08	06
Sep 10	Sold more one Bushill more of Rye	00	03	02½
	~~Sold a Load of Rye Strawe~~			
	~~Sold three pecks of Wheat at home~~	~~00~~	~~04~~	~~02~~
	Totall of what I made of Rye *[£8 0s 6½d]*	07	18	08½
	Sold three pecks of wheat at home	00	04	02
Jul 17	Carried to Ellstree one bushill & ½ a peck of wheat	00	06	04
Sep 10	Sold at Hartford two Loads of Wheat	02	16	00
8	Sold at Hartford three loads of Wheat	04	07	00
1	Sold at Hartford one Quarter of Oates	00	15	06
8	Sold at Hartford three Quarter of Oates	02	03	06
Sep	Sold one Load of Pease	00	18	00
	Used one Quarter of Oates my selfe	00	15	00
7	Sold two Bushills of Pease	00	06	00
7	Sold three Loads of Wheat & Rye Strawe	01	01	00
22	Sold at Hartford three Quarter of Oates	02	04	00
25	Brought to Ellstree two Loads of wheat	02	12	00

---

[11] Lower case 'h' written originally
[12] *idem*: the same
[13] Other sales suggest that 'sowed' meant 'sold' in this context

	Item[14] to Ellstree one load of Pease	00	15	00
	Item one Quarter of Oates	00	14	08
	Item eight Bushill of Chaffe	00	02	00
Sep 29	Sold at Hartford eight Loads of Wheat	10	06	00
	Item two Quarters of Oates	01	09	04
5	Sold at home three Loads of Pease	01	16	00
6	Sold at home seven Bushills of Wheat	01	15	06
	I have two Loads of Pease in the House by me[15]	01	00	00
	Sowed one load of Wheat upon the Glebe Land	01	05	00
Oct 20	Sold at Hartford 4 Loads of Pease	02	10	00
	One Load of Fetches [16] & two Quarter of Oats	02	01	00
	[£50 3s 6½d]	51	03	08½

[6] An Account of moneys received at Datchworth 1711

Oct 6	Sold two Porketts[17] at ~~Hartford~~ home for £2 8s 6d which cost me £1 7 s 0d remains neat [18] profitt	01	01	06
Oct 21	Sent into Hartford eight Quarter of Barley at	08	04	00
	Spent one Quarter of Oates in the stable	00	15	00
	Sold one Quarter of Oates to Welwyn	00	15	00
	Spent 3 Bushils & 3 Pecks of Miscellane in the House[19]	00	15	00
Oct 26	Sold to Jeaques one Quarter of Oates at	00	15	00
	Item twelve Bushills of Chaffe	00	03	00
	Item some Pease strawe I have at	00	02	00
	Sent to Ellstree 80 Bushills of Chaffe	01	00	00
	Sold one Load of Pease to John Bassett junr	00	12	06
	~~Sold to Jeaques~~	~~00~~	~~00~~	~~00~~

---

[14] The use of the word 'item' here is not clear. It may have been used instead of '*idem*'.
[15] The shillings entry could be '2' or '0'.
[16] fetches: vetches
[17] porket is a young pig
[18] 'neat' is an obsolete version of 'net'
[19] 'miscellane' or miscellany was a mixture of wheat and rye that provided flour for bread called 'maslin' (Ernle, *English farming past and present,* p8)

TITHE ACCOUNTS

Oct 27	Sold at Hartford three Quarter & 6 Bushills of Oates	02	15	09
	Item two Load of Pease	01	04	06
Oct 29	Dressed up for my Own horse one Quarter of Oates	00	14	06
	Sold William Whittenborough 3 Bushill of Pease	00	07	06
	Sold one Load of Wheat Strawe	00	08	00
30	Sold Naysh two Bushill & 3 Pecks of Miscellane	00	11	00
31	Sold John Bassett senior 2 Loads of Pease	01	05	00
Nov 3	Sold at Hartford 3 Loads of Wheat	03	18	00
	Item sold two Loads of Pease	01	03	00
	Item brought to Ellstree one load of Wheat	01	05	00
	Item brought 40 bushills of Chaffe	00	10	00
Nov 17	Sold at Hartford ten Quarters of Barley	10	05	00
	Used at Datchworth myselfe 6 Bushill of Oates	00	10	09
	Brought to Ellstree at several time 1 Quarter of Oates	00	15	00
Dec 16	Sold at Hartford eight Loads of Wheat at 1.7.0	10	16	00
	Killed a fat Hog which cost me in 1.4.0 and which was worth 2.10.0 so the profit is	01	06	00
[1711/12]				
Jan 19	Sold at Hartford 5 Quarter & ½ of Barley for	06	01	00
Jan 23	Brought to Ellstree 2 Loads of Wheat	02	14	00
[1711]				
Dec 23	Sold at Hartford 2 Loads of Wheat	02	14	00
[1711/12]				
Jan 27	Brought to Ellstree 1 Quarter of Oates	00	15	00
	Item three Sacks of Chaffe	00	*[blank]*	
	Killed then another Hogg which cost me in 1.4.0 and was worth 2.15.0 so the profit is	01	11	00
	Sold Naysh 6 Bushill of Pease at	00	15	00
	Sold Tyler one Load of Pease at	00	12	06
	Total received	67	00	06

[7] An Account of moneys received at Datchworth 1711

1711/12

Feb 19	Sold at Hartford 6 Quarter of Oates at 14sh 8d the Quarter	04	14	00
	Spent one Quarter more on Oates at home	00	14	08
Feb 12	Sold then at Datchworth 112 B[ushe]l of Chaffe at 3d	01	08	00
Feb 23	Sold at Hartford 6 Quarters of Oates & 2 Bushills	04	16	07
	Sold to Jeakes 4 Bushill of Oates	00	07	10
Feb 26	Francis brought home \to Ellstree/ 1 Load of wheat	01	08	00
	Item 3 Bushills of Pease	00	07	06
	Mr Pinkney has had 4 Bushill & ½ of Pease	00	11	03
	One Bushill of wheat	00	05	06
	One stack of wood	00	12	00

[1712]

Mar 25	Naysh has had since a peck of blew Pease [20]	00	01	00
	Tyler has had since a Bushill & halfe of Pease	00	03	03
	Titmasse has had 3 Bushills of Pease	00	07	06
	Mr Tomson had a Load of Pease	00	12	06
	Michael Ray had one Bushill of Pease	00	02	06

2 Fatt Hogs eat 3 Loads of Pease £1 17s 6d.
3 Piggs eat 7 Bushills of Pease £0 17s 6d. These three piggs cost me in together the sum of £1 2s 0d ~~Sold them for £3 10s 0d~~ which with 7 Bushills of Pease is £1 19s 6d. Sold them for £3 1s 0d profit remaining is[21]   01 11 06

Sowed my selfe 4 Bush[e]l of Pease	00	10	00
Sowed six Bushill of Oates	00	11	03
Sowed 2 Bushill of Blew Pease	00	08	00
Sowed eight Bushill of Barley	01	00	00
Sold 12 Bushill more of Barley	01	10	00
James has had 2 Bushill & halfe of wheat	00	13	09

---

[20] blew pease: 'blue peas', common or garden peas (Bristow, *Glossary*, p17)

[21] If his profit is correct, he sold the 'hogs' for £3 10s rather than £3 1s.

Mar 29	Brought to Ellstree 2 Loads & 1 Bushill of wheat	03	01	06
	Sold the tythe wood in Adams's wood for	00	05	00
Apr	Sold Jeakes 9 Bushills of Chaffe	00	02	03
	Sold him 3 Bundles of strawe	00	00	09
	Sold him a peck of pease	00	00	10
	Sold William Whittenborough Tythe Wool being two Tod[22]	01	05	00
	[In a different hand, possibly Hawtayne's son]	27	11	11

$$51 \ 3 \ 8$$
$$67 - 6$$
$$\underline{27 \ 11 \ 11}$$
$$145 \ 16 \ 11$$

[[**8**] *has been placed after* [**4**]]

[9] *Composition agreements 1712*

An Account of those persons who have hired their Tythes of me for three years, that is to say, from Midsummer 1712 to Midsummer 1715 at the Rates that are set against their several Names as Underwritten, and by agreement that the Money for the said Tythes shall be due so soon as the Corn & Crop is Ended, after which the Day of Payment for the said Money agreed for is left to the appointment of Mr Hawtayne.

Those that are crossed pd Dec 1st 1712 [*Note in margin*]			££ sh dd
In p[ar]t	5 10 0	William Blindall in Datchworth X	11 10 00
		William Emmins of Knebworth X	03 10 00
		Daniell Crawley in Datchworth X	03 10 00
		William Deardes of Knebworth X	01 10 00
		John Millard of Welwyn X	00 10 00
		William Whittenborough in Datchworth X	04 10 00
In p[ar]t	2 05 0	John Whitfield in Datchworth X	04 10 00
In p[ar]t	2 10 0	Robert North in Datchworth X	05 00 00
		John Tompson in Datchworth X	16 00 00
		Thomas Catlin in Welwyn X	01 13 00

[22] One tod is about 28 lbs

		John Phips in Datchworth X	00 05 00
		William Pennyfather in Welwyn X[23]	05 00 00
		William Pendred in Datchworth X	00 12 00
		Michael Ireland in Datchworth X	01 00 00
		Thomas Venables in Datchworth X	00 04 06
In p[ar]t	2 10 0	John Randall in Datchworth X	05 00 00
		Widowe Kimpton in Welwyn X	01 00 00
		William Hatton in Datchworth X	01 00 00
		Edward Grey in Datchworth X	00 02 06
		John Mansell in Datchworth	00 04 00
		Robert Mardall in Datchworth X	00 03 00
In p[ar]t	6 15 0	John Flindall in Knebworth X	09 10 00
		Edward Mardell of Woolmore Green X	00 12 00
		John Venables in Datchworth X	00 04 00
		John Basset junior X	00 08 00
		John Flindall in Datchworth	00 13 00
		William Cater of Aston	00 02 00
		John Bigg of Aston	00 02 00
		[£ 78 5s 0d]	66 5 0

[10] *Probably an abandoned attempt to list more composition agreements.*

~~We whose names are hereunder written do agree to pay Mr Hawtayne those several sums of money that are set in figures against our Names on the other side of this Leave and upon the terms that are there mentioned~~

~~Edward Pennyfather seven shillings Yearly~~	00	07	00
~~Mr Halloway~~	00	10	00

John Whitfield's land holding and how he was farming it in 1715.

An Account of the Land in Datchworth Parish belonging to Hopper's End Farm formerly belonging to Mr Kidall now in the possession of one Mr Hawkings Brewer in London and at present in the Occupation of John Whitfield

Crop of Tilt this present Year 1715[24] [*Four roods = one acre*]

	Acre	
Shop Keeper's Close[25] is in all 2 Acres	1 & ½	plowed

---

[23] This amount was originally entered as £4, then changed to £5.

[24] Tilt (tilth) crop was wheat and/or rye sown on previously fallowed land. Edge (etch) crop followed tilt and was barley and oats and/or peas and beans.

2 Fields by Church Grove	4	plowed
1 Piece in Cundell Common	1	1 Rood
Acres Field by Painter's Green	4	plowed
A Field belowe that	2	plowed

[*Total Tilt*] 12 [Acres] 3 Roods

Edge Crop this present Year 1715		
Brome Field by Painter's Green	3	plowed
The Field belowe that	3	
Lillys Ware called 7 is but	6	
White's Brome called 6 is but	5 ½	
The Orchard Field	6	
Rag House Field	4	

[*Total Edge*] 27 ½ [Acres]

Fallow this present Year 1715		
Old Field in Datchworth called 7 is	6	plowed
Daniells Field	2	plowed
Daniells Mead	2	

[*Total Fallow*] 10

[*27 ½ has been overwritten by 28*] 28

12 3 [Roods]

[*Total of John Whitfield's land holding*] 50 [Acres] 3 Roods

[11] *Parishioners and their land holdings (undated). A third column, headed 'Pole', was not used by Hawtayne so has been omitted.*

	Acres	Roods
Audleys Farm in Burnham Green Lane lately in the Occupation of John Ipgrave. Consists of an house Homestall[26] + 30 or 28 Acres of land divided into Eight Fields	30	
Thomas Freeman of West End holds of Rowland Mardell at West End an House & Homestall and 11 or 12 Acres of Land as he told me	12	

---

[25] Shopkeepers Close, Acres Field, and Orchard Field, are on the 1839 tithe map, field numbers 388, 342 and 394 respectively (HALS: DSA4/34/2)

[26] homestall: ground immediately connected with the house

TITHE ACCOUNTS

Michael Ireland rents of Joseph Caughton of Hartford an House 2 Orchards consisting both of halfe an Acre and 12 Acres of Land divided into six intire Closes in this Parish. One Close part in Tewin and part in this Parish. 3:4th Parts of the Close in this Parish. This House commonly called the White House. 12

Mote House Farm in this Parish and Seven Acres of the Land in this Parish, now in the Occupation of Robert Winch Tennant to Sir Thomas Clerk 07

Edward Grey rents an house at Govers Green with 2 Orchards consisting one Acre in this Parish the Landlord is William Thorp. 01

John Cater rents an House of S[i]r Thomas Clerk at Govers Green with an Orchard of 1 Acre near 01

Benjamin Uncle & Widowe Ansell live in an House at Govers Green rented of Nathaniel Page the Orchard consists of one Acre 01

Edward Pennyfather rents an House of William Pennyfather in Burnham Green Lane with 4 Acres of Land 04

Mr Hollows lives in his own House in Burnham Green Lane and holds 10 Acres of Land in his own hand, which is all that belongs to the said House 10

[12] *Parishioners and their land holdings (continued)* Acres Roods

John Venables holds an House in Burnham Green Lane with an Orchard & 2 Closes consisting of five Acres Hedge and Ditch 4 or 4½ plowing Land 05

Mr Audley owns an house in Burnham Green Lane with 30 Acres of Land adjoyning all in this Parish 30

John Ginn lives in an house of his own in Burnham Green Lane with an Orchard and two Acres of Land adjoyning 02

Daniel Ginn lives in an house in the same Lane with an Orchard and a Close of one Acre rented of George Naysh who lives at London   01

Thomas Venables lives in an House at Bulls Green with 4 Acres of Land adjoyning rented of Thomas Naysh of Burnham Green   04

John Smith lives in an house of Capt[ai]n Thomas Adams at Bulls Green with one Acre of Land adjoyning   01

John Crawley lives in an House at Burnham Green with an Orchard & a Mead adjoyning consisting of near an Acre rented of Capt[ai]n Thomas Adams   01

William Bigg and [*blank*] Ballard live in an House at Burnham Green divided into two Tenements with an Orchard adjoyning consisting of halfe an Acre   00   02

Daniel Mardell lives in an house called the Pond House by Hawkins Hall with an Orchard adjoyning consisting of ½ an Acre   00   02

William Butterfield lives at the Farm called Hawkins Hall belonging to Mrs Knight of Wellwin and has 7 Closes[27] in this Parish consisting of 50 Acres of Land or thereabouts
Green End[28] 10 Acres 9 plowd, 6 Acres next Painters Green Lane, Pond Field 10 Acres, Tunnel 10 Acres, Dovehouse Field 10 Acres, meadow & Little Field 4 Acres with the Orchard   50

Edward Mardell of Woolmore Green holds 3 Acres of Land in this Parish lying near Swangleys   03

James Blindall of Woolmore Green hold Acres of Land in this Parish   [*blank*]

---

[27] The number '7' has been written over either 'six' or 'sev'.
[28] Great Green End, Pond Field, Turnhill and Dovehouse Field are on the 1839 tithe map numbered 321, 348, 227 nd 346 respectively (HALS: DSA4/34/2)

[13] *Parishioners and their land holdings (continued)*	Acres	Roods
Thomas Catlin \of Woolmore Green/ holds 12 Acres of Land in this Parish	12	
John Hawkins near Woolmore Green holds 15 Acres of Land in this Parish	15	
Thomas Miller of West End holds 5 Acres of Land in this Parish	05	
William Dardes of Dardes End holds 45 Acres of Land in this Parish [*blank*] Acres in Busticle Common[29] [*blank*] Acres in Oak Field Common and 3 inclosed Fields lying near Oak Field in all 45 or 40 Acres	45	
William Emmins of Broadwater holds 85 Acres of Land in this Parish of Esq Lytton lying from Broadwater on Each side the Green Lane and on Each side Oke Field Lane all inclosed Fields	85	
William Pennyfather of Harmer Green holds of his own Land in this Parish called the Bulls consisting of 25 Acres; as also other Lands belonging to the Farm he lives in at Harmer Green. The 2 Perry Fields one of them consisting of 30 Acres, the one of 20 the other of 10 so he has in all in this Parish[30]	55	
Rowland Mardells Farm now in his own hands consists of 41 Acres and an halfe of Land as Underwritten	41	02
2 Closes called Rockleys ag[ain]st the Church with some woodland adjoining[31]	15	
One Acre in Chibden Common	01	
The upper Field next the Lane by Church Grove	03	

---

[29] Busticle Common cannot be identified (see also **[14]**). The fact that it is referred to as land held by a resident of Deards End may mean that it is the earlier name for one of the commons on the Knebworth side of Datchworth parish.

[30] Fields 440, 444, 464 and 466 all contained 'Bulls' in their names on the 1839 tithe map. Great Perrys, 448, is the relic of the two fields mentioned (HALS: DSA4/34/2)

[31] Tilbury Rockley, Upper Rockley and Nut Croft are numbers 222, 223 and 343 respectively on the 1839 tithe map

The Middle Field	03
The Lower Field next above the Yard	06
Nutt Croft	03
Field over the High Way ag[ain]st the House	04
The Meadow above the House	04
The Close by Tit[masse]'s [32] house at the hither End of Datchworth Green	02: ½
	41: ½

[14] *Details of land associated with Swangleys Farm and Raffin Green Farm (undated), and finally, William Ives' holdings, dated 1727.*

Swangleys Farm	Acres	
Robert Flindall & his B[rothe]r Samuel hold of Mr Lytton 1 Fryer Field[33] 16 Acres, 13 in Datchworth, 2 in Nebworth[34]	13	
Winch Croat 3 Acres bare measure	3	
Miles Rays Ley 9 Acres	9	
Little Fryer Field 2 Acres	2	
Great Pinkoe 14 Acres some in Nebworth	14	or 12
Stoney or Little Pinkoe \10 Acres/ some in Nebworth	5	
Brome Close 6 Acres [6 *has replaced 3 in both cases*]	6	
Mead by the House 2 acres	2	
Olly Pitts 14 Acres	14	or 12
Oake Field 3 Acres	3	
Busticle Common 4 Acres [*Could be 3 or 4*]	3	

---

[32] The name is difficult to decipher. It could be 'Tibs' (there is no-one called 'Tib' or 'Tibs' elsewhere) or a shortened form of 'Titmasse' as suggested

[33] Of the land associated with Swangleys Farm the following fields are on the 1839 tithe map: Friar Field (258), Wench Croft (287), Ray's Ley (288), Great Pinker (92), Stoney Pinker (141), Great Clay Pits (85) (possibly 'Olly Pitts'), Great Pullans (280) and Baines's (147-151) (possibly Barns's), (HALS: DSA4/34/2)

[34] 16 has replaced 12 and both 13s have replaced 10

Hilly Cloase 4 Acres [*4 has replaced 2 in both cases*]	4
1 Close belowe the House Grunhill Hill	3
1 Close above the House	[*blank*]
Great Pullens [*12 has replaced 14*]	12
Barnes's	25
Of Captn Adams in our Common [*1½ has replaced 3*]	1½
	117½

William Kimpton's Land which he holds of Robert King Esq	
Laune[35] ten Acres. If not 12 Acres	10
Stock Close four Acres & ½ or 5	04½
Hoppett two Acres[36]	02
Cole Wood Close	05
2 Little Closes of Stephen Uncles	02½
Godberry	05
2 Swangleys	15
	44

William Ives holds in this Parish 1727

Of the Widowe Nash's Land 22 Acres

Of Youngs Land

Of Mr Kings Land twenty Acres

[15] An Account of what corn I sold at Datchworth from Midsummer 1712 to Midsummer 1713

1712

Aug 9	Sold at Hartford Market 2 Loads of wheat at	02	12	00
16	Sold at Hartford 5 Loads of wheat at	05	10	00

---

[35] Two fields called The Lawn existed in 1839 (209 & 220)

[36] The Hop Pit (212), Little Godbury (202) and Little & Upper Swangleys (225, 226) are on the 1839 tithe map (HALS: DSA4/34/2)

	Sold then at home 4 Bushill and halfe of Miscellane to Bigg & Naysh & Titmasse at	00	14	03
23	Sold at Hartford 2 Loads of wheat	02	00	00
26	Brought to Ellstree 1 Load of wheat at	01	00	00
	and one Load of Miscellane at	00	15	00
	Thrashed for my Horses 4 Bushill of Oates	00	06	00
27	Sold to Mardell the Smith a Bush[e]l of Miscellon	00	03	00
30	Sold at Hartford 4 Load of wheat at 19 sh	03	16	00
	Sowed at Datchworth 2 Bushill of Miscellane[37]	00	06	00
Sep 3	Carried to Ellstree 12 Bushill of Oates	00	18	00
	Used at Datchworth 1 Quarter of Oates more	00	12	00
9	Sold Titmasse one Bushill of wheat	00	03	10
20	Sold at Hartford 7 Loads of wheat at	06	10	06
	Sowed at Datchworth 5 Pecks of wheat	00	04	00
23	Brought to Ellstree 1 Load of wheat	00	18	06
	Brought one sack of Chaffe	00	01	00
	Brought 4 Bushill of Aples	00	04	00
Oct 18	Mr Tompson sold 3 Loads of Miscellane \& 3 Pecks/ at	02	00	05
25	He sold at Hartford 7 Quarter + 6 B[ushe]l of Barley at 16sh 6d the Quarter	06	07	10
Nov 14	Sold to Ware 8 Quarter + ½ of Barley at 17sh + 6 per Quarter	07	08	09
	Sold to Big ~~one~~ two Bushill of Miscellane at	00	05	06
15	Brought to Ellstree 4 Bushill + 3 Pecks of Wheat at	00	19	00
	Brought one Load of Miscellane at 12sh 6d	00	12	06
	Brought two Quarter of Oates at 11sh the Quarter	01	01	00
	Brought 3 sacks of Chaffe at 3d a Bushill	00	02	03
	Brought one Bushill of Barley Light Corn	00	01	09
	Sold my Turnips on the Glebe at Datchworth for	03	15	00
29	Sold at Hartford 3 Loads of Misling	01	19	00

---

[37] 'Sowed' means 'sold' in this context. This is consistent with sales of similar crops

Dec 3	Sold to Hewson 3 Bushill and a Peck of Miscling[38]	00 08 08
	Sold to Mardell the Smith 3 B[ushe]l of Miscellane	00 08 00
		52 03 09

[16] An Account of what corn I sold and what moneys I received at Datchworth from Midsummer 1712 to Midsummer 1713

		£ sh d
1712	Brought from the other side	52 03 09
Dec 3	Sold to Big the Tasker 2 B[ushe]l + 1 Peck of Misling	00 06 07
	Goodman Big had before one Bush[e]l of misling	00 02 07
1712/13		
Jan 7	James Pendred sold five Load + 3 Bushill of Pease	02 16 00
	Item 3 Quarter of Oates at 12 sh per Quarter	01 16 00
1713		
Jun 17	Sold Tythe Wood to Thomas Goose for	01 05 00
	Sold Tythe Wood to Mardell the Black Smith	00 12 00
		59 01 11

[17] Charges at Datchworth in the year 1712 from Midsummer 1712 to Midsummer 1713

1712

Aug 9	Charges at Hartford when sold 2 Loads of wheat	00 00 10
16	Charges at Hartford when sold 5 Loads of wheat	00 01 10
23	Charges in carrying 2 Load wheat to Hartford & selling it	00 02 03
23	Pd William Big for thrashing in all [17s has replaced 14s]	00 17 02
30	Charges at Hartford when sold 4 Loads of wheat	00 01 06
	Pd to Boys at Plowe & Dung Cart & going to Hartford	00 03 00
	Pd to my Tything man for the Harvest 1712	02 12 06

---

[38] miscling, another version of maslin, mixture of wheat and rye, see [6]

	Pd to Thomas Naysh for his Labour in Harvest	02	10	00
	For 6 Bushill of Malt for bear in harvest	00	[blank]	
	Have had of Mr Tompson 5 p[oun]d of Turnip seed at 3d	00	01	03
	For his carrying 2 Loads of Wheat to Hartford	00	01	08
Sep 20	Sold at Hartford 7 Loads of wheat at	06	10	06
23	Brought to Ellstree 1 Load of wheat	00	18	06
	Brought 4 Bushills of Aples to Ellstree	00	04	00
Sep 20	Charges at Hartford when sold 7 Loads of wheat	00	02	09½
Oct 18	Charges by Mr Tompson for carriage & empting of 7 Quarter and six B[ushe]l of Barley & the 3 Load of Misling	00	09	02
Nov 14	Charges when sold 8 Quarter + ½ of Barley to Ware	00	[blank]	
[1712/13]				
Jan 7	Charges when sold 5 L[oa]ds etc of pease & 3 Quarter of Oates	00	[blank]	
	Charges for horse hire which Francis Blindall left [4s 6d has replaced 3s 8d]	00	04	06
	[Total, excluding deleted amounts]	[7	8	5½]

[18] From Mid Summer 1713 to Midsummer. 1714

An Account of my Receipts at Datchworth concerning only the Glebe Land and what Tythes I had then in my own hand which were William Kimpton's Tythes of Mr Kings Farm at Raffin Green which Thomas Coulson held before which was let at 04:10:0 per Annum
And Ipgraves Tythes which used to be let at 02:0:0
And Chapmans Tythes which used to be let at 01:4:0
And Thomas Jeakes's Tythes which were only 1 Acre
And Elliots Tythes which were not quite 2 Acres 00:04 0

Sold as Underwritten the Grain of the Glebe Land and those Tythes

1713		£	sh	d
Sep 19	Sold at Hartford 4 Loads of Rye at 16sh the Load	03	04	00
	Sold then one Load of Wheat at	01	05	00

TITHE ACCOUNTS

Sep 26	Sold at Hartford 3 Quarter of Oates at 16sh only 6d bated[39]	01	15	06
	Sold then one Load of Pease at 12sh 9d	00	12	09
Oct 3	Sold at Hartford 4 Loads of Pease at	02	02	06
	Sold Goodman Titmasse at home ~~one~~ \halfe/ a B[ushe]l of Pease	00	01	00½
	Sold Ipgrave the Tasker 3 B[ushe]l of Rye at	00	10	00
	Sold Goodman Naysh 6 B[ushe]l of Rye at	00	19	06
Oct 12	Received of Farr the Butcher for Tythe Apples	00	01	00
	Received of Michael Ray for his Tythes	00	01	06
	Sold one Bushill of Wheat to Farr the Butcher at	00	06	00
	Sold one B[ushe]l of Wheat to Mardell the Smith	00	05	06
	Sold Turnips to Capt Adams for £3 15sh: 0	03	15	00
	Brought one B[ushe]l of Barley to Ellstree	00	02	06
	Brought one B[ushe]l of Rouncifull[40] Pease to Ellstree	00	02	06
Oct 21	Sold Naysh the Clerk 2 B[ushe]l of Wheat at 4sh	00	08	00
	Sold one to Ipgrave the Tasker	00	04	00
	Received then of Goodm[a]n Crawley for 4 Quarter & 6 B[ushe]l of Barley which he sold the Saturday before at Hartford	04	15	00
	Brought then to Ellstree 2 B[ushe]l of Oates	00	03	04
	John Brought since to Ellstree 1 B[ushe]l of Barley and one of Pease	00	04	00
Dec 7	John Brought to Ellstree 2 B[ushe]l of Oates	00	03	04
	Sold to Mr Waller[41] 4 B[ushe]l of Oates	00	06	08
	Sold George Harding one B[ushe]l of Pease	00	02	06
[1713/14]				
Jan 5	Sold Ireland 3 B[ushe]l of Pease and two of Tares	00	10	00
6	Sold Naysh one B[ushe]l of Pease at 2sh	00	02	00
7	John brought home 2 B[ushe]l & ½ of Oates	00	04	02

---

[39] 'bated' means rebated

[40] 'rouncival' describes a kind of marrow-fat pea

[41] Possibly a curate, see [22] and see Introduction: People in the Parish, Curates

Sold Naysh the Clerk formerly one Load of Pease	00 11 00	
	22 18 3½	

[19] Charges at Datchworth in the year from Mid Summer 1713 to MidSummer 1714

1713			£ sh d
Sep	19	Charges at Hartford in carrying & fetching 4 L[oa]ds of Rye 1 of Wheat	00 07 01
Sep	26	Charges there when sold 3 Quarter of Oates & 1 L[oa]d of Pease	00 05 06
Oct	3	Charges there when sold 4 L[oa]ds of Pease	00 05 02
	3	Goodman Naysh received for Ending the Crop	03 05 00
		Flindall for his Horse and Cart	00 14 00
		For the Hire of a horse T.	00 05 06
		Pd for Howing of the Turnips	00 18 00
Oct	21	Pd Goodman Ipgrave the Thrasher	[blank]
[1713/14]			
Jan	5	Pd Goodman Harding for Cutting of Chaffe	00 05 00
		Pd him for Thrashing	[blank]
		[Total]	[06 05 03]

[20] Composition agreement: Thomas Goose 1713

I do hereby agree ~~from~~ to hire the Tythes of the Lands which I now hold in the Parish of Datchworth in the County of Hartford of Mr William Hawtayne Rector of the said Parish for three years commencing from Michaelmasse[42] last past before the Date of these presents; as also of the Land belonging to the ~~Land~~ House which William Cowper now lives in, and which Land is also in the Occupation of the said William Cowper being by Estimation four Acres; For the Tythes both Great and small, of all which Lands, I do hereby agree and Promise to pay to the said Mr William Hawtayne the sum of twenty pounds Yearly, for Each and Every of the said three Years commencing from Michaelmasse last past as is above said which sum of twenty pounds I do hereby acknowledge to

---

[42] Michaelmas, 29 September

be due to the said Mr William Hawtayne as soon as the crop shall be taken off from the ground or Ended in Each and Every of the said three Years. And the first twenty pounds which will be due when this present crop now upon the ground shall be Ended I do promise hereby to pay it to Mr William Hawtayne in the manner following that is to say one ten pounds on or before the 29th Day of October next Ensuing the Date hereof and the other ten pounds on or before the Feast of St Thomas[43] next Ensuing the \Date/ Hereof as Witnesse my Hand this third Day of August in the Year of our Lord 1713

Tho Goose [*signed*]

Witnesse hereto   A Smythe, William Walles [*signed*] [*Total*] £20 0s 0d

one Acre & halfe of Land which Thomas Skegg holds by the smith's shop is included in this agreement

[21] *Composition agreement: William Wallis[44] 1713*

I do hereby agree to hire the Tythes of the Lands which I now hold in the Parish of Datchworth in the County of Hartford of Mr William Hawtayne Rector of the said parish for three years commencing from Michael[ma]s last past before the Date of these presents; For which Tythes both great and small I do hereby agree and promise to pay to the said Mr William Hawtayne the said sum of Eight pounds and ten shillings Yearly for Each and Every Year of the said three Years, which sum of Eight pounds and ten shillings I do hereby acknowledge to be due to the said Mr William Hawtayne Each and Every Year so soon as the Crop shall be taken off removed from from the Ground, or Ended; and which said sum of Eight pounds and ten shillings which will be due to the said Mr William Hawtayne for this crop which is now upon the ground and which will be Ended this present Harvest, I do hereby agree and promise to pay it to the said Mr William Hawtayne on or be in manner following that is to pay four pounds and five shillings one moyety thereof on or before the 29th Day of Octr next Ensuing the Date hereof and four pounds and five shillings the other moyety on or before the Feast of St Thomas next Ensuing the Date hereof as Wittnesse my Hand this third Day of August in the Year of our Lord 1713 and so on for Every and Each of the said three Years By me

William Walles [*signed*]

Witnesse Hereto   A Smythe, Tho Goose [*signed*] [*Total*] £8 10s 0d

---

[43] St Thomas, 21 December

[44] William Wallis owned Datchworth manor from 1693 until 1719 (see Appendix 2)

[22] November 2nd 1713 Received of the Several Persons as underwritten in part for their Tythes due at Michaelmasse last past

Nov	Received of Thomas Adams three pounds in part X[45]	03	00	00
	Received of William Blindall in part X	05	15	00
	Received of William Emans in full XX	03	10	00
	Received of William Whittenborough in part	02	05	00
Dec 14	Received of Edward Mardell in full X	00	06	00

An Account of the Particular Moneys that I received January 4th 1713/4 when I made a feast to the Parishioners

Jan	4	Received of John Flindall by the common in full X	00	13	00
		Received of Susanna North in full X	05	00	00
		Received of Thomas Goose in full X	20	00	00
		Received of Rowland Mardell for Mrs Randall in part	04	10	00
		Received of Thomas Venables in full	00	04	06
		Received of John Venables in full	00	04	00
		Received of Thomas Miller in full	00	10	00
		Received of Thomas Freeman in part	00	16	00
		Received of William Pennyfather in full	04	00	00
		Received of Daniell Crawley in part	03	02	00
		Received of John Bassett sen	00	01	08
		Received of John Bassett jun	00	10	00
		Received of John Phip	00	05	00
	5	Received of Robert Flindall of Swangleys in part	07	05	00
	6	Received of Mrs Kimpton of Mardley Berry in full X	00	08	00
	6	Received of John Tompson in part	15	00	00
		Received of William Blindall more in part	02	10	00
	5	Received of Thomas Adams more	00	08	00
		Received of William Wallis by order given to Daniel Crawley	04	05	00

---

[45] The crosses may be related to checking against composition agreements

	Received of him before by order to Mr Waller X	04	05	00
	Received of John Whitfield in part	02	05	00

1714

Jun 7	Received of William Dardes in full X	01	10	00
	Received of Michael Ireland one p[oun]d in full for tythes	01	00	00
	Received then also of Mr Holywell in full	00	10	00
Jul 3	Received then also of Michael Ireland for halfe a years rent for the Parsonage House and Glebe Land due at Lady Day[46] last past five pounds	05	00	00
	Received then of William Whittenborough in full	02	05	00
	[£101 3s 2d]	96	02	06

[23] *Continuation of receipts 1714*

Jul 31	Received then of Rowland Mardell more for Mrs Randall	00	10	00
Aug 10	Michael Ireland Received of Daniel Crawley for my use	00	08	00
	Ditto Received of Thomas Kimpton for Ditto	00	12	00
Sep 9	I received of John Whitfield more in full of 1713	00	07	06
Dec 19	Received of Edward Grey	00	02	06
	[£2 0s 0d]	01	18	00
	[£101 3s 2d]	96	02	06
	Totall made in 1713 [£103 3s 2d]	98	00	06

[24] An Account of my Receipts for Tythes at Datchworth due upon the Harvest 1714

Oct 9	Received of John Whitfield for great Tythes	04	02	06
11	Received of William Emmins in full	03	10	00
11	Received of John Flindall by the Common in full	00	13	00
15	Received of William Whittinborough in part	04	02	00

---

[46] Lady Day: 25 March

16	Received of Susanna North Widowe in part	02 00 00
16	Received of Michael Ireland in part of Michaelmas rent	02 03 00
28	Received of William Wallis ~~in part with a bad Crown Piece~~	04 05 00
28	Received of Thomas Goose senr in part by money and taxe pd	10 00 00
Nov 1	Received of Daniel Crawley for Great Tythes only	03 02 00
1	Received of Joshua Flindall in part	04 15 00
1	Received of Michael Ireland for Rent of Glebe Land & House	02 17 00
1	Received of William Hatton in full to Midsummer next	01 00 00
1	Received of Thomas Adams for the Tythe of 16 Acres & ½ of L Cn [47] [*16 has replaced 17*]	01 16 00
Nov 22	Received of John Tompson in part for Capt Wallis	05 00 00
22	Received of Rowland Mardell on part	03 05 00
22	Received of Susanna North Widowe more in part	01 10 00
Dec 17	Received of Thomas Goose senr in full more	10 00 00
Dec 18	Received of William Dardes in full	01 10 00
Dec 19	Received of Robert Winch the sum of one pd in full	01 00 00
Dec 20	Received of John Phipp ~~the~~ in full	00 05 00
Dec 20	Received of John Tompson more in part	09 00 00
Dec 20	Received of Thomas Catlin in full	01 13 00
Dec 21	Received of Edward Grey in full to Midsummer last	00 02 06
Dec 21	Received of Thomas Venables ~~the~~ in full	00 04 06
Dec 21	Received of Susanna ~~Harwood~~ North Widowe in full	01 10 00
Dec 21	Received of William Pennyfather in full	03 00 00
Dec 21	Received of Rowland Mardell in full for Mr Randall	01 15 00
Dec 21	Received of William Blindall in money then besides five p[oun]ds paid before to Mr Betham[48]	10 00 00

---

[47] The tithe of about 2s per acre suggests edge crop. The abbreviation 'L Cn' could be short for 'latter corn' meaning 'second corn' (OED). Adams paid tithe for 16 ½ acres of 'tilt' in 1719 **[37]** which would be consistent with edge in 1714 using a 3-year rotation

[48] Mr Betham was curate from 1714. See **[73]**

Dec 21	Received of John Miller in full	00	10	00
Dec 21	Received of Mrs Rebecca Kimpton in full	00	12	00
21	Received of Thomas Freeman in full	00	08	00
21	Received of Benjamin Uncle in full	00	04	00
1714/15 Feb 3	Received then of John Farr the sum of four shillings for the tythe of some Turnips which he sold for forty shillings, and eight shillings for his other great and small Tythes, in the presence of Goodman Ireland senr and Dame[49] Ireland his son's Wife	00	12	00
	[*£96 6s 6d*]	96	07	06

[25] An Account of Tythes due upon the harvest 1714

1715

Jun 6	Received of William Pendred	00	12	00
	Received of [*blank*] Mansell	00	05	00
	Received of John Bassett junr	00	10	00
	Received of Ireland my Tennant for Kimpton's Tythe	00	17	06
	Recd of Ireland for Ipgraves Tythes	02	08	00
	Recd of Ireland for James Blindall's Tythe	00	02	00
	Recd of Ireland for Captn Adams Tythes	00	09	00
	Recd of him in money which he collected of several people for their Tythes	00	14	00
Jun 28	Received of more of William Blindall in full	01	10	00
28	Received of John Tompson more in part	01	00	00
28	Received of John Whitfield in full	00	07	06
28	Received of Daniel Crawley in full	00	08	00
Aug 8	Received of Edward Grey to Midsummer last	00	02	06
9	Received of John Ginn	00	01	06
9	Received of Mr Hollows ten shillings	00	10	00
10	Received of Thomas Goose senr in part for Mr King's Tythes	01	05	00
	Received of Michael Ireland last Lady Day's Rent	05	00	00

---

[49] dame: the mistress of the household

	Received of Robert Flindall formerly at several times for the Tythes of Swangley's Farm which his Mother Holds	04	15	00
12	Received of the R[ev]d Mr Eyres[50] for 3 Acres in Catchpole Field for two Years	00	16	00

1716

Nov 20	Received of John Bassett senr[51]	00	01	08
1716/17 Feb 2	Received of Mr Miles for Capt Wallis for a former Year[52]	02	00	00
		23	14	08
	[£96 6s 6d]	96	07	06
	[£120 1s 2d]	120	02	02

[26] *Composition agreement: Robert Flindall 1715*

Memorandum It is hereby agreed between William Hawtayne Rector of Datchworth in the County of Hartford and Robert Flindall of the said Parish, that he the said Robert Flindall shall have, hold, possesse and End all and all Manner of Tythes as well the Tythes of all Manner of Corn, as the Tythe of Turnips and all other small or petty Tythes growing upon arising from or belonging to the Lands which Joanna Flindall Widowe, Mother of him the said Robert Flindall dos now rent or hold in the said Parish for three Years next Ending at the feast of St Michael which will be in the Year of our Lord 1717. He Paying for Each and Every of the said three Years to him the said William Hawtayne the sum of nine pounds and ten shillings, the first payment of nine pounds and ten shillings to be made on or before the feast of St Michael next Ensuing the Date hereof and so on for every one of the said three years. In Witnesse whereof both Partys have set their hands this 29th Day of July in the Year of our Lord 1715
Robert Flindall   his mark   [*marked*]   Willm Hawtayne   [*signed*]
Witnesse hereto   John Bassett   [*signed*]
£9 10s 00d

---

[50] Revd Christopher Eyre, Rector of Aston from 1700 until his death on 9 May 1743 in Winchester (HALS: DP9/1/1)

[51] This entry may be retrospective. See **[30]**, entry for John Bassett, same date and amount

[52] Another retrospective entry. See **[29],** the entry for Mr Miles on the same date

TITHE ACCOUNTS

[27] *Composition agreement: William Blindall 1715*

Memorandum It is hereby agreed between William Hawtayne Rector of Datchworth in the County of Hartford and William Blindall Yeoman of the said Parish that He the said William Blindall shall hold his Tythes both great and small arising in the said Parish; as well as the Tythe of Turnips as all Manner of other Tythes for three Years commencing from Michaelmasse last, and Ending at the Feast of Saint Michael which will be in the Year of our Lord 1717, He the said William Blindall paying for the same to him the said William Hawtayne ~~for~~ at the Feast of St Michael in Each Year Every Year of the said three Years the sum of Eleven pounds and ten shillings; The first payment to be made at or upon the Feast of St Michael next Ensuing the Date hereof, and so on the Feast of St Michael for Every Year of the said three Years. In Witnesse of which agreement they do both set their Hands this twenty Eig[h]th Day of June in the Year of our Lord 1715. Provided always that He the said William Blindall shall hold or Rent or Occupy no more or other Lands than what he dos at present Occupy and Possesse.

William Blindall   his mark   [*marked*]   Willm Hawtayne   [*signed*]
Witness hereto   Mikel Irelad Senr [*signed*]   Michel Ierland Junr [*signed*]
[*Total*] £11 10s 0d

[28] An Account of Tythes due upon the Harvest 1715

	Received of Thomas Goose in part	05	00	00
	Received of Thomas Goose in part	05	00	00
Aug 20	Received of William Emmins in full	03	10	00
Sep 14	Received of William Whittenborough in part	03	02	06
Nov 8	Received of William Whittenborough in full	01	07	06
	Received of William Hatton upon Account	00	18	00
	Received of Robert Winch ~~the~~ one pound in full	01	00	00
	Received of John Phipp in full	00	06	00
	Received of William Wallis in part	04	05	00
	Received of Daniel Crawley in full	05	00	00
	Received of William Pennyfather in part	02	00	00
	Received of John Flindall in full	00	13	00
	Received of Robert Flindall in [*blank*]	09	10	00
Nov 9	Received of William Blindall in part	06	10	00

		£	s	d
	Received of Thomas Goose more in part	09	00	00
	Received of William Kimpton in part	03	00	00
10	Received of John Miller in full	00	10	00
	Received of William Butterfield in part	03	00	00
	Received of Robert King Esq in full to Midsummer last	01	05	00

[*note on left hand facing page*] Bragher End paid Latter Marth[53] to Mr Hawtayne *vide contra*[54] Took of Mr King in Kind 12 li[55] of Hops Dried & one Load of Latter Marth Hay and 6 Dozn of Peaches & Nectarins. Valued the Hops at £1 4s 0d, the Hay at £1 0s 0d, the fruit at 4s

		02	08	00

[1715/16] Receivd of Edward Mardell of Woolmore Green in
Jan 9 p[ar]t 8 sh[56]

		£	s	d
Jan 9	p[ar]t 8 sh[56]	00	12	00
	Receivd of William Pendred in full	00	12	00
	Receivd of John Pharr in part	00	09	06
	Receivd of James Blindall for one Acre of Oates	00	02	00
	Receivd of John Smith of Bulls Green by his Wife	00	01	06
	Receivd of William Butterfield more in full	02	00	00
	Receivd of William Pennyfather more in full	02	00	00
	Receivd of Thomas Catlin in full	01	04	00
	Receivd of Thomas Goose senr in full	06	00	00
	Received of William Wallis by the Tax Bill	04	05	00
	Received of Thomas Adams for 1 Acre and ½ of Vetches	00	03	00
	Receivd of John Bassett junr in full	00	10	00
	Receivd of Thomas Flint in full	00	10	00
	Received of John Whitfield for Great Tythes	05	06	00
10	Received of Francis Bigg	00	03	00

---

[53] 'latter marth' is a version of 'aftermath', the herbage remaining after the hay harvest (Coleman and Wood, *Glossary of Terms*, p9)
[54] '*vide contra*': 'see opposite'
[55] This may be 'li', the abbreviation for '*librae*', pounds (see Appendix 7)
[56] 8 shillings is not consistent with the amount entered

Received of William Blindall more in part	03	10	00
	89	13	00

[29] An Account of my Receipts upon the Harvest 1715

1715/16

Jan 11	Received of Thomas Freeman in part	00	15	00
	Receivd of Michael Ireland for Tythes at the White House	00	17	00
	Receivd of him halfe a years Rent at Mich[aelma]sse	05	00	00

1716

Apr 12	Received of Mr Hallows to Michaelmasse last	00	10	00
13	Recd of Thomas Venables senr to ditto	00	04	00
	Received of William Blindall in full	01	10	00
	Recd of Widow Kimpton upon Acct	00	10	00
Aug 31	Received of Thomas Venables junr	00	04	00
	Received of [*blank*] Mansell by his Wife	00	05	00
Oct 14	Received of the Widowe Kimpton more in full	00	06	00

1716/17

Feb 2	Received of Mr Miles for small Tythes	01	10	00
		11	11	00
	Brough[t] from the other side	89	13	00

1715/16

		101	04	00
Jan 9	more in full one pound seventeen shillings[57]	01	17	00
		103	01	00

Sales of corn 1715

Sold of the Crop 1715 *Imprimis* 1 Load of Wheat	01	01	06
Sold three Load more of Wheat at 15sh	02	05	00
Sold 7 Quarter of Barley at 19sh per Quarter	06	13	00
Sold 9 Loads of Wheat at 18sh per Load	07	02	00

---

[57] This entry and the final one on [29] appear to have been added later and seem to be a repeat of the same item, ie William Kimpton's tithe. The year may be 1715/16, a retrospective entry made to be included with the other entries made on Jan 9 [28].

Sold 3 Loads of Wheat at 19sh per Load	02	17	00
Sold 19 Bushill of Barley at 2 : 0 : 4	02	00	04
Sent to Ellstree 3 Loads of Wheat at 17sh 06	02	12	06
Sent to Ellstree 2 Loads of Miscellane	01	05	00
Sent to Ellstree 7 Bushill of Pease	00	17	06
Thrashed and Eat myselfe 5 Quarter & ½ at 13sh per Quarter	03	11	06
Sold at Datchworth 9 Bushill of Pease	01	02	06
2 Bushill of Miscellane	00	07	00
	31	14	10
	101	04	00
1715/16	132	18	10
Jan 9 William Kimpton as above	01	17	00
	134	15	00

[30] An Account of my Receipts of Tythes upon the Harvest 1716

	William Whittenborough	04	10	00
	Daniell Crawley in part	04	00	00
Sep	William Pennyfather in part	02	03	00
	Of John Flindall in full	00	13	00
Nov 19	Received of William Hatton in full	01	00	00
19	Received of William Butterfield for 15 Acres of Tilt Crop and 20 Acres of Edge Crop and five shillings for small Tythes	05	05	00
19	Received of William Pendred in full	00	12	00
19	Received of William Kimpton 8 Acres of Tilt 32½ of Edge	05	09	00
19	Received of John Whitfield 9 Acres of Edge 8 of Tilt	03	00	00
19	Received of John Bassett junr in full	00	10	00
19	Received of Daniel Crawley in full	01	00	00
20	Received of John Bassett senr	00	01	08

TITHE ACCOUNTS

20	Received of Rowland Mardell for Turnips in the Year 1715	00	10	00
	Received of him for other small Tythes	00	12	06
	Received of him for Tythe Turnips in the Year 1716	00	17	00
	Received of him for other small Tythes to Mich[aelma]s 1716	00	12	06
1716/17 Feb 1	Received of him for his Uncle and Aunts Funeral in the Chancell	04	00	00
	Received of Edward Mardell of Wolmore Green for 3 Acres of Edge corn	00	06	00
	Received of Thomas Goose in full the sum of £20	20	00	00
	Received of William Wallis in full	08	10	00
	Received of Thomas Catlin in full	01	04	00
	Received of Thomas Flint in full	00	10	00
	Received of John Millard in full	00	10	00
	Received of Edward Mardell 3 Acres of Edge	00	06	00
	Received of James Blindall 2 Acres of Tilt 1 of Edge	00	10	00
	Received of John Farr in full	00	15	00
	Received of Mr Hallows	00	10	00
	Received of Thomas Freeman	01	01	00
	Received of Thomas Venables	00	04	00
	Received of Mr Miles for small Tythes	01	10	00
	Received of him for Turnips upon the Glebe	03	00	00
Feb 14	Received of William Pennyfather in full for 20 Acres Tilt	01	17	00
	Received of Joseph Mansell	00	05	00
	Received of Edward Pennyfather	00	07	00
	Received of Benjamin Uncle in part	00	05	00
	Received of John Venables	00	04	00
	Received of Widowe Mardell in part for 6 Years	00	05	00
Feb 18	Received of Thomas Adams[58]	03	05	00

---

[58] In the original document, this entry came after the entry for John Smith below.

1717

Sep 30	Received of John Smith of Bull's Green	00 01 06
	[£80 1s 2d]	80 11 02

[31] *Continuation of receipts of tithes upon the Harvest 1716*

1716	Received of Mrs Rebecca Kimpton[59]	00 16 00
Sep 13		
	Brought from the other side [£80 1s 2d]	80 11 02
	[£80 17s 2d]	81 17 02

An Account of what I made of the Tythes which I ended in the Year 1716

Sold 6 Loads of wheat at 24 shillings the Load		07 04 00
~~11 Qr and halfe of Barley sold it in the whole for~~[60]		[*illeg*]
7 B[ushe]l of Tares sold		00 13 02
12 Lds of Pease at 11 sh [*illeg*][61]		06 10 00
2 B[ushe]l & halfe of Beans		00 05 00
13 Quarter of Oates at 12sh per Quarter		07 16 00
		~~29 04 02~~
Wintering of 3 Cows		02 00 00
11 Quarter and halfe of Barley at 18sh the Quarter		10 09 00
		34 17 02
[*Possibly meant to be £81 17s 02d from above*]		81 11 02
		116 08 04

[32] An Account of my Receipts upon the Harvest 1717

Sep 30	Received of John Flindall thirteen shillings	00 13 00
	Received of Daniel Crawley	05 00 00
	Received of John Smith of Bulls Green	00 01 06

---

[59] Probably a retrospective entry

[60] The amount appears to have been overwritten, deleted and then re-entered below

[61] This entry is difficult to decipher. 'Lds' (Loads) appears to overwrite 'Qr' (Quarter). The rate looks like 11s, though the total should be £6 12s. Rates for 'pease' vary, but 11s per load is of the right order

TITHE ACCOUNTS

Oct 1	Received of William Whittenborough	04	10	00
	Received of Thomas Adams senr for Wood in part	00	14	00
Oct 4	Received of the Revrd Mr Eyres[62] for Catchpole 3 \Acres/ Tilt	00	12	00
5	Received of John Whitfield	06	02	06
Oct 19	Received of Mr Hallows	00	10	00
	Received of Robert Flindall in part	01	05	00
	Received of William Blindall in part	04	00	00
Nov 4	Received of William Pendred	00	10	00
	Received of William Wallis in part	03	14	06
5	Received of John Miller in full	00	10	00
5	Received of William Butterfield in part	02	03	00
5	Received of William Kimpton in part	02	12	00
	Received of Sir Thomas Clerk's Bayley[63]	01	00	00
Nov 25	Received of Thomas Goose senr in part	10	00	00
	Received of William Emmins in part	01	01	06
Dec 9	Received of John Smithe of the White House[64]	01	00	06
	Received of Edward Grey	00	02	06
	Received of Benjamine Uncle in part	00	05	00
	Received of Thomas Venables senr by Joseph Baldock	00	04	00
Dec 10	Received of Robert Flindall more in part	03	10	00
	Received of William Pennyfather in full	04	00	00
Dec 16	Received of Thomas Goose more in full	10	00	00
	Received of William Wallis more in full	04	15	06
	Received of John Venables junr in full	00	08	00
Dec 28	Received of William Butterfield more upon account	01	07	00

---

[62] Revd Christopher Eyre, Rector of Aston, 1700 to 1743

[63] baily: a contraction of bailiff; one who would oversee the running of a manor or an agricultural estate

[64] The two John Smiths are distinguished here according to location. There is a 'White House' in Datchworth but it was built after this period.

Dec 28	Received of Thomas Freeman for 4 \Acres/ of Tilt & 5 \Acres/ of Edge	01	01	00
30	Received of William Emmins more in full	02	08	06
	Received of John Gurney for nine years	00	02	07
	Received of Robert Flindall the sum of in full	04	15	00

He has not given me Captn Adams's Receipt for 9:10:0
the Year before so he owes me for that Year till that
Receipt is Deliverd

[1717/18]

Feb 18	Received of Thomas Adams upon account	02	00	00
	Received of Nathaniel Barnett for a Tythe Pigg	00	02	00
	[£81 0s 7d]	79	02	07

[33] *Continuation of receipts upon the Harvest 1717*

1717/18

Mar 5	Received of John Bassett for himself	00	10	00
Mar 8	Received of him for his Father	00	01	00
	Received of Thomas Hills to Michaelmasse last	00	03	00
	Received of Joseph Mansell	00	07	06
1718 Apr 10	Received of William Blindall	07	10	00
Jun 2	Received of William Kimpton more upon Acct	00	08	00
	Received of John Mardell for himself and Mother	00	07	00
Aug 14	Received of John Ginn	00	02	00
Nov 4	Received of Alice Kimpton Widowe for 6 years ending at Micha[e]l[ma]se	00	12	00
1718/19 Jan 2	Received of Edward Mardell of Woolmore Green	00	06	00
1719 May 8	Received of Mr William Miles for a Years small Tythes due Michaelmasse 1717	02	00	00

	[£12 6s 6d]	12	09	06
Brought over	[£81 0s 7d]	79	02	07
The 1st sum total belowe amounts to	[£93 6s 1d]	91	12	01

	29	05	09
	120	17	10
My Charges in the Year 1717 were[65]	[051]	05	03
	[59]	12	07
Rent of the Glebe	10	00	00

Sold of the Tythes in the Year 1717

Sold 9 Load and 1 Bushil of Wheat at £1 1s a Load	09	13	00
Thrashed and eat myselfe 1 Quarter of Pease	00	16	06
Dards's Oates 2 Quarter & 5 Bushil at 12sh the Quarter	01	11	06
9 Quarter of Barley sold for seven p[oun]ds	07	00	00
13 Loads of Pease at 10sh a Load	06	10	00
2 Loads & three Bushill of Tares	01	06	00
4 Quarter of Tythe Oates	02	08	00
	29	05	00

Made of the Crop upon the Glebe Land 1717

Sold 7 Loads & 2 Bushill of Rye at 13sh 9d the Load	05	01	09
10 Quarter of Barley off from the Walnutt Tree Piece	09	00	00
9 Loads of Wheat	09	00	00
2 B[ushe]l and an halfe of Rye	00	05	00
13 Loads of Pease at 10sh a Load[66]	06	10	00
6 Quarter & 5 Bushill of Oates	04	00	00
4 Ld & 2 Bushill of Pease	02	04	00
	29	10	09

[34] *Continuation of receipts upon the Harvest 1717*

The first sum total on the left page **[33]** is	12	09	06
The 2d [*second*] sum brought over is	79	02	07
Sold the Tythes I took in kind for	29	05	00

---

[65] These two entries have been overwritten but these and other deletions have been entered accurately on **[34]**

[66] This deleted entry appears in the 'Sold of the Tythes', 1717, immediately above

	The Rent of the Glebe Land	10	00	00
	Total of Profitt is	130	17	01
	My Expenses in that Year were	051	05	03
	Rests in Money	79	09	10
1725	Received of Rowland Mardell for the Tythe of			
May 17	Turnips and other small Tythes	01	00	00

[35] Receipts of Tythes due upon the Harvest and at Michaelmasse 1718

Sep 29	Received of Mr Hallows ten shillings	00	10	00
Oct 1	Received of Captain Thomas Adams	00	16	00
8	Received of William Whittenborough for 53 Acres	05	06	00
15	Received of Daniel Crawley	05	00	00
20	Received of John Godfrey at the Mote House	01	00	00
21	Receivd of William Pendred in part	00	08	00
27	Received of John Farr in full	00	14	00
28	Received of William Wallis in part	04	05	00
Nov 3	Received of Rebecca Kimpton for 4 Acres of Oates	00	08	00
4	Received of John Smith at the White House on Acct	01	00	00
4	Received of Thomas Venables senr in full	00	04	00
4	Received of Alice Kimpton Widowe for 4 Acres of Land and her small Tythes	00	10	00
10	Received of Thomas Goose senr in part for Tythes	05	09	04
	Received of ditto for 2 Years Rent due at Mich[ae]l[ma]se 1718 of a Piece of Glebe in Hallington Meadow	00	02	06
1718				
Dec 22	Received of William Kimpton in full	04	10	00
[1718/19]				
Jan 1	Received of Thomas Goose senr in full	14	10	08
Jan 2	Received of Edward Mardell of Woolmore Green	00	06	00
Jan 2	Received of Edward Grey in full to Midsummer last	00	02	06
Jan 2	Received of William Wallis in full to Michaelmasse last	04	05	00
2	Received of Samuel Flindall for Turnips on the Glebe	04	10	00

	2	Received of John Whitfield	05	00 00
	14	Received of William Dardes for small Tythes	01	05 00
		Received of him for one Acre and halfe of Rye	00	06 00
		Received of William Emmins for small Tythes	01	01 00
		Received of Samuel Flindall for small Tythes	01	01 00
	15	Received of John Mardell	00	13 00
	16	Received of William Blindall for small Tythes	02	00 00
	17	Received of John Miller	00	10 00
	17	Received of William Pendred in full	00	04 00
	17	Received of Thomas Adams junr for 1 Acre & ½ of Pease	00	03 00
1719 May 8		Received of Mr William Miles for a Years small Tythes due at Michaelmasse 1718	02	00 00
1719 May 12		Received of William Pennyfather for one Years small Tythes due at Michaelmasse 1718	01	01 00
		Received of [blank] Williams by Nash at Michaelmasse 1718	00	01 06
1719 Jun 29		Received of William Butterfield by Receipts for Poor Rate and Taxes	05	00 00
			74	02 06
[1719] Sep 28		Received of Edward Pennyfather[67]	00	07 00

[36] *Continuation of receipts of Tythes due at Michaelmasse 1718*

1718 Nov 3		~~Received of Mrs Rebecca Kimpton for 4 Acres of Oates~~[68]	~~00~~ 00	~~06 00~~ 08 00
1719 Oct 17		Received of Francis Blindall due Mich[aelma]sse 1718 for his small Tythes of 20 Acres of Land	00	10 00
Oct 26		Received of Joseph Mansell	00	05 00
		[*includes deleted 8s of Mrs Rebecca Kimpton*]	01	03 00
		Brought over	74	09 06

---

[67] In darker ink, this was a retrospective entry added when Edward Pennyfather paid 7s on Sep 28 in the 1719 tithe collection [37]

[68] Repeat of entry on [35], hence deduction lower down [36]

	Total	75	12	06
	Rent of the Glebe	10	00	00

1720

Jul 20	Received of Edward Mardell of Woolmore Green[69]	00	06	00
	Deduct 8 shillings Received of Mrs Rebe[c]ca Kimpton for 4 Acres of Oates as being twice charged	00	08	00
		09	18	00
		75	12	06
		85	10	06

1725 May 17	Received of Rowland Mardell for Turnips and other small Tythes[70]	01	00	00

[37] Payments of Tythes let & due Sept 29:1719 & June 24 1719

	Received of Thomas Hills due at Midsummer	00	02	00
Sep 19	Received of Edward Grey due at Midsummer	00	02	06
21	Received of Captn Thomas Adams	00	14	00
28	Received of Edward Pennyfather	00	07	00
Sep 29	Received of John Mardell	01	05	00
Oct 2	Received of Thomas Adams for 16 Acres & ½ of Tilt on Account	03	06	00
2	Received of Mr Hallows	00	10	00
13	Received of Nathaniel Asser for Mr Audley's Land	01	14	00
	Received of William Pennyfather	05	00	00
17	Received of William Whittenborough	04	14	00
17	Received of William Dardes	02	05	00
17	Received of Francis Blindall for small Tythes only	00	10	00
26	Received of Joseph Mansell	00	05	00
26	Received of Daniel Crawley	05	00	00
28	Recd of Joseph Hudson for that which William Hatton did hold	01	08	00
Dec 21	Received of John Miller	00	10	00

---

[69] This appears to be a retrospective entry added when the 1720 tithe was paid, **[37]**
[70] This entry appears for several years up to the 1724 return, **[42]**

	Received before of William Butterfield	05	00	00
[1719/20]	Received of John Whitfield for the small Tythes of			
Jan 27	Hoppers End Farm	00	07	06
	And for Benjamin Uncles Tythes	00	05	00
1719/20				
Mar 6	Received of John Venables the sum of	00	08	00
6	Received of Thomas Venables senr	00	06	00
[1720]				
Apr 13	Received of Thomas Williams in full for a Year	00	02	00
14	Received of John Farr in full for a Year by a Bill	00	14	00
	Received in Novr 1719 of William Kimpton	04	10	00
May 4	Received of Mr Miles for small Tythes in full to			
	Michaelmasse last 1719	02	00	00
	John Hawkins	01	04	00
	Received of Robin Flindall in part for small Tythes	01	00	00
		43	09	00
Jul 20	Received of Edward Mardell of Woolmore Green	00	06	00
22	Received of Francis for his Uncles James Blindall	00	06	00
1720/1	Recd of Robin Flindall for the small Tythes of			
Jan 29	Datchworth and Knebworth in which I take of Mr			
	Lytton the Rector[71]	02	00	00
Apr 13[72]	Received of Thomas Goose for the Tythes of eleven			
	Acres of Turnips sold to William Hall of Amwell			
	which Turnips grew in Mr Kings Field called			
	Eatington[73]	01	10	00
Jun 23	Received of William Wallis in part for small Tythes &			
	Turnips	00	15	00
26	Received of William Blindall for small Tythes &			
	Turnips	01	00	00
	Received more of William Wallis in full for small			
	Tythes	00	15	00

[71] The Revd William Lytton was rector of Knebworth from 1704, (Venn, J & J A, *Alumni Cantabrigienses*, (Cambridge, 1924) vol III, p92

[72] This group of entries may be retrospective, but the year of payment is not obvious in this case

[73] This field name is not on the 1839 tithe map but it was mentioned in an Abstract of title as 'Eatenden' in 1702 (HALS: DEAS/1595)

		50	01	00
1725 May 17	Recd of Rowland Mardell for Turnips & other small Tythes	01	00	00

[38] Payments of Tythes due at Michaelmasse 1720

Sep 30	Received of John \Phipp/ as by agreement	00	10	00
Oct	Received of William Pennyfather	05	00	00
Nov 8	Received of John Godfrey	01	00	00
9	Received of Daniel Crawley	05	00	00
9	Received of William Whittenborough	04	14	00
9	Received of Joseph Hudson	01	10	00
9	Received of John Smith	01	02	00
22	Received of little John Smith for 3 Years	00	04	06
22	Received of Widowe Pendred in part	00	05	00
30	Reced of John Mardell for West End	01	05	00
	Recd of him for ½ an Acre of Tilt in the Common	00	02	00
Dec 20	Received of William Butterfield in full	05	00	00
21	Received of William Kimpton in full	04	10	00
21	Received of Alice Kimpton Widowe in full	00	10	00
29	Recd of Thomas Venables senr in full	00	05	00
29	Recd of Nathaniel Asser in full	02	08	00
29	Recd of Thomas \Adams/ junr in full	02	00	00
[1720/1] Jan 2	Recd of John Titmasse by the Common in ~~full~~ part	00	13	00
2	Recd of Robin Flindall for small Tythes in Datchworth and Knebworth the which I take for Mr Lytton Rectr of Knebworth	02	00	00
	Recd of Mr Ludnam for that which was Mr Hallows's	00	10	00
Jan 30	Received of Thomas Venables junr	00	06	00
	Received of John Venables	00	08	00
Feb 10	Received of Thomas Millard	00	10	00
[1721] Apr 5	Received of Thomas Field for 9 Acres of Turnips & other small Tythes	00	10	00

13	Recd of Thomas Goose for small Tythes	01	00	00
May 13	Recd of John Blindall	00	06	00
17	Recd of Edward Pennyfather	00	07	00
25	Recd of William Wallis in part for small Tythes & Turnips	00	15	00
26	Recd of William Blindall in part for small Tythes & Turnips	01	00	00
Jul	Recd more of William Blindall in full for small Tythes & Turnips	01	00	00
	Recd more of William Wallis in full for small Tythes & Turnips	00	15	00
Jul 24	Recd of Edward Grey to Midsummer last 1720	00	02	06
1721				
Oct 30	Recd of Mr William Miles for small Tythes	02	00	00
1725 May 17	Recd of Rowland Mardell for Turnips & other small Tythes[74]	01	00	00

[Total] [48 08 00]

[39] Recd upon Acct for Great & Small Tythes due in the Year Ending at Michaelmasse 1721

Jul 1 1721	Received in part of William Whittenborough	04	00	00
	Received of Goodman Smith in part for Small Tythes	01	10	00
	Recd of William Blindall in part for Small Tythes	01	01	00
	Recd of Robin Flindall for a Tythe Lamb	00	05	00
	Recd of him for Tythe Wool & Grasse[75]	00	06	06
Jul 24	Recd of Edward Grey to Midsummer 1721	00	02	06
Aug 7	Recd of William Butterfield in part	02	10	00
Aug 11	Received of John Field in part	04	04	00
Aug 16	Received of Mr Charles Jones in full	00	10	00
Oct 3	Recd of William Pennyfather in full for Tythes	05	00	00

---

[74] Different ink confirms that this has been added later.
[75] 'grasse' probably referred to the payment for grazing. See also 'herbage' [70].

3	Recd of Mr William Miles for small Tythes	02	00	00
6	Recd of William Whittenborough more in full	00	14	00
	Recd of John Field more in full	01	01	00
26	Recd of William Butterfield more in full	02	10	00
30	Recd of John Smith at the White House	01	02	00
30	Recd of John Godfrey	01	00	00
Nov 16	Recd of Thomas Adams of Welches	02	00	00
23	Recd of William Kimpton	04	10	00
Dec 6	Recd of Daniel Crawley	05	00	00
6	Recd of Joseph Hudson	01	10	00
[1721/2]				
Jan 7	Received of John Venables	00	08	00
14	Received of John Ginn	00	02	00
15	Recd of Thomas Venables junr	00	06	00
17	Recd of Thomas Venables senr	00	06	00
17	Recd of Nathaniel Asser	02	08	00
Feb 10	Recd of Edward Pennyfather	00	07	00
Apr [1722]	Received of Joseph Mansell	00	05	00
Apr 21	Received of Thomas Miles	00	10	00
	Received of William Dardes by his Bill for meat	02	05	00
	of Robert King Esq	02	00	00
	of John Hawkins	01	08	00
	of Mardell of Woolmore Green	00	06	00
	of James Blindall of ditto	00	06	00
1722	Received of Mr William Hall for the Small Tythes			
Jul 12	of Swangleys due at Mich[aelma]sse 1721	01	14	00
Oct 21	Received of John Crawley upon Acct	00	01	00
	Recd of Joseph Baldock	00	02	00
1725	Recd of Rowland Mardell for Turnips & other small			
May 17	\Tythes/	01	00	00

[Total] [54 10 00]

[40] Payments of Great & small Tythes due in the Year Ending at Michaelmasse 1722

1722	Received of William Whittenborough in part for great etc	04	04	00
Jul 23	Recd of John Goose in part for small Tythes	01	01	00
24	Recd of James Whitehall upon acct for small Tythes for the Berry Farm	02	00	00
25	Recd of Henry Smith in part for small Tythes	01	10	00
Sep 15	Recd of Mr Thomas Adams of Walkerne	00	16	00
18	Recd of Joseph Hudson in full	01	10	00
	Recd of John Eylett in part	00	10	00
	Recd of John Field in part	02	10	00
Oct 15	Received more of John Field in full	02	15	00
	Received of Thomas Adams of Welches upon Account	02	00	00
20	Received of John Crawley one shilling and a Tythe Pigg	00	03	00
22	Received of William Butterfield	05	00	00
Nov 30	Recd William Bedell for small Tythes	00	04	00
Dec 1	Received of Thomas Venables junr	00	06	00
Dec 3	Received of William Wallis for small Tythes	01	10	00
3	Recd of Henry Smith more for small Tythes	00	05	00
3	Recd of William Whittenborough more in full	00	10	00
[1722/3]				
Jan 1	Recd of Nathaniel Asser in full	02	08	00
5	Recd of Thomas Venables senr	00	06	00
5	Recd of John Venables	00	08	00
	Recd of William Pennyfather of Harmer Green for small Tythes	02	00	00
19	Recd of Edward Pennyfather	00	07	00
	Recd of Joseph Baldock	00	02	00
Feb 3	Recd of Thomas Harwood for a Year	00	03	00
28	Recd of Daniel Crawley in full	05	00	00
28	Recd of [*blank*] Kirby for a Years Tythes	00	04	00

1723

Sep 30	[*blank*]of John Hawkins	01	08	00
Sep 30	Received of John Farr	00	10	00

1723/4

Jan 6	Received of Joseph Webster in full[76]	00	15	00
	Received of Mr Dardes	02	05	00
	Received of John Bassett	00	05	00
	~~Received of Titmasse by the Common~~	~~00~~	~~16~~	~~00~~

1725 May 17	Recd of Rowland Mardell for Turnips & other small Tythes	01	00	00

[*Total excluding deleted amount*] [*43 15 00*]

[41] Receipts for Tythes for the Year 1723 Ending and due to me at Midsummer and Michaelmasse in the Parish of Datchworth

Sep	25	Received of John Goose for Small Tythes	02	00	00
	26	Received of James Whitehall for Small Tythes	02	00	00
Oct	4	Received of Captn Thomas Adams of Walkerne	00	16	00
	4	Received of Thomas Adams of Welches for all his Tythes	02	00	00
	4	Received of Henry Smith for Small Tythes	01	15	00
Sep	30	Received of John Farr in full	00	10	00
		Received of Joseph Hudson in full	01	10	00
Oct	7	Received of Mr Charles Jones in full	00	10	00
	11	Recd of William Pennyfather in full	05	10	00
		Recd of William Whittenborough in full	04	14	00
Oct	19	Recd of William Butterfield in full	05	00	00
		Received of Daniell Crawley in full	05	00	00
		Received of long John Smith in full	01	00	00
		Received of Venables John	00	08	00
		Received of Thomas Venables junr	00	06	00

---

[76] A retrospective payment, see same date [41]

	Received of Thomas Kimpton of Swangleys Small Tythes	01	15	00
Jan 1[77]	Received of Daniell Mardell of Woolmore Green	00	06	00
[1723]				
Dec 31	Received of Jane Hawkins Widowe	01	08	00
Dec 30	Received of John Eylett	01	12	00
	Received of Nathaniel Asser in part	*[blank]*		
	Received of Edward Grey	00	02	06
	Received of John Kirby	00	05	00
	Received of Richard Hewson	00	03	00
	Received of John Phipp	00	10	00
[1723/4]				
Jan 6	Received of Joseph Webster in full	00	15	00
Jan 7	Received of Joseph Miller	00	10	00
Feb	Received of John Bassett	00	05	00
	Received of *[blank]* Titmasse by the Common	00	16	00
	Received of William Dardes	02	05	00
	Received of William Kimpton	04	10	00
[1724]				
May 2	Recd of Richard Ansell for 3 Years to Easter 1724	00	02	00
	Recd of William Wallis for Small Tythes to Michaelmasse last	01	10	00
1725				
May 17	Recd of Rowland Mardell	01	00	00
	[Total]	*[50*	*13*	*06]*

[42] Receipts of Tythes for the Year 1724 Ending and due to me at Midsummer & Michaelmasse in the Parish of Datchworth

Sep 29	Received of Joseph Hudson	01	10	00
Oct 23	Received of Thomas Kimpton of Swangleys for Small Tythes	02	00	00
23	Received of Thomas Adams of Welches	02	00	00

---

[77] Probably 1723/4

24	Recd of John Field	05	05	00
24	Recd of Mr John Luddenham for Land late Mr Jones's	00	10	00
	Recd of James Whitehall in part for Small Tythes	02	00	00
26	Recd of Daniell \Crawly/ for Bragher End Farme Small Tythes	02	00	00
	Recd of him for Nashes Land the Small Tythes	01	00	00
26	Recd of John Smith of the White House	01	02	00
27	Recd of William Emmins for Small Tythes	01	01	00
27	Recd of William Kimpton in full	04	10	00
Nov 28	Recd of John Eylett in full	01	12	00
Oct 31	Recd of William Butterfield in full	05	00	00
	Recd of William Pennyfather in full	05	10	00
Dec 1	Received of William Whittenborough	03	12	00
	Received of John Phipp	00	10	00
Dec 21	Recd of Mr Thomas Adams of Walkerne	00	16	00
22	Recd of John Miller	00	10	00
26	Recd of John Farr	00	10	00
26	Recd of Richard Hewson	00	02	00
28	Recd of John Venables	00	08	00
29	Recd of John Goose for Small Tythes	02	00	00
	Recd of John Titmasse for great & small	00	16	00
	Recd of Thomas Nash of Bragher End for all Tythes	00	10	00
[1724/5]				
Jan 15	Recd of John Freelove	01	04	00
Jan 18	Recd of Joseph Webster	00	16	00
Mar 22	Received of William Wallis	01	10	00
	Received of Peter Culver	00	05	00
	Recd of [blank] at Burnham Green	00	02	00
1725				
May 17	Recd of Rowland Mardell in full	01	00	00
May 17	Recd of Thomas Hills for one Year Ending at Mich[aelma]sse last	00	02	00
	For the Tythes of Barnes Closes in my Occupation	02	10	00

	For the Tythes of Mrs Hawkins Land in my Hands	02	00	00
1727				
Nov 21	Received of ~~Geo~~ Daniel Mardell[78]	00	02	06
Jan 24	Received of Edward Mardell of Woolmore Green	00	06	00
	[Total]	[54	11	06]

[43] Payments of Tythes due at Midsummer and Mich[aelma]sse 1725 at Datchworth

Oct	5	Received of Thomas Adams of Walkern for Woods	00	06	00
	12	Received of Joseph Hudson	01	10	00
	12	Received of Thomas Adams of Welches	02	00	00
		Received of ~~Mr~~ Robert King Esq	07	05	00
		of John Field	05	05	00
		of John Ilett	01	12	00
		of John Smith	01	02	00
		of William Pennyfather	05	10	00
		of Nathaniel Asser	02	12	00
		of William Emmins	06	00	00
		of John Miller	00	10	00
		of [blank] Franklin's son in Lawe	01	04	00
		of Daniel Crawley for small Tythes	02	15	00
		of John Goose for small Tythes	02	00	00
		of William Wallis for small Tythes	01	15	00
		of Thomas Nash of Bragher End for small Tythes	00	07	00
		of John Titmasse for small Tythes	00	07	00
		of William Whittenbury	04	00	00
		of James Whitehall for the Berry small Tythes	03	00	00
		of Thomas Venables for Tythes	00	06	00
		of John Venables	00	08	00
		of John Freelove	01	04	00

---

[78] Both Daniel and Edward Mardell's entries were in a different ink, so added later

	of John Phipp	00	10	00
May 1726	of William Blindall for all Tythes	11	00	00
	Received of William Butterfield	05	10	00
	Received of John Pierce	01	00	00
Jun 14	Received of Thomas Kimpton	12	00	00
	of Mr Luddenham	00	15	00
	of William Dardes	02	05	00
	of John Blindall of Woolmore Green	00	06	00
	of Edward Mardell of Woolmore Green	00	06	00
1727				
Nov 21	Received of George Ray[79]	00	07	00
	Received of Daniell Mardell	00	02	06
[1727/8]				
Jan 24	Received of Thomas Hill	00	02	00
	[*Total*]	[*85*	*01*	*06*]

[44] 1727[80]

Sep 15	Received of William Butterfield in part	03	10	00
	Received of Thomas Adams of Welches	02	00	00
Oct 1	Received of James Whitehall in part	10	00	00
	Received of Thomas Kimpton in full	12	06	00
16	Received of Mr Daniel Haynes	00	10	00
	Received of William Pennyfather in full	05	10	00
	Received of John Smith in full	01	02	00
	Received of Capt Thomas Adams in full for Woods	00	06	00
	Received of William Ives	05	05	00
	Received of William Whittenbury	03	15	00
	Received of John Field	05	05	00
	Received of Joseph Hudson	01	10	00

[79] Both George Ray and Thomas Hill appear to be retrospective entries. See [44]
[80] Between [43] and [44] there is a blank page headed 1726 with no entries

	Received of John Ilett	01	12	00
	Received of Edward Pennyfather	00	07	00
17	Received of John Phipp	00	10	00
25	Received of William Butterfield in full	05	00	00
	Received of Daniel Crawley for Small Tythes	02	00	00
	Received of Thomas Venables six shillings	00	06	00
Nov 14	Received of the Widowe Whittenbury	00	16	00
18	~~Received of Thomas Venables~~	~~00~~	~~06~~	~~00~~
	Received of John Venables	00	08	00
	Received of William Emmins	06	00	00
Nov 20	Received of Francis Kimpton	00	01	00
21	Received of George Ray for Rowland's Land	00	06	00
	for his own Land	00	01	00
Dec 1	Received of John Miller	00	10	00
	Received of Thomas French	01	04	00
Dec 26	Received of William Blindall	11	00	00
	Received of James Whitehall more in full	10	00	00
	Received of Joseph Webster	00	15	00
	Received of Christopher Draper for Small Tythes	00	10	00
	Received of Daniel Mardell by Richard Blindall	00	02	06
	Received of Mr Luddenham by Richard Blindell	00	15	00
	Received of William Wallis for Small Tythes	01	15	00

[1727/8]

Jan 24	Received of Thomas Hill the Blacksmith	00	02	00
	Received of Edward Mardell of Woolmore Green	00	06	00
	Received of Joseph Baldock	00	02	00

[*The following entry is on the back of* **[44]**]

[1728]

Apr 27	George Langley paid due Mich[aelma]sse	00	02	00
	[*Total excluding deleted amount*]	[*95*	*09*	*06*]

[45] Tythes due at Michaelmasse & Harvest 1728

Sep 30	Received of William Whittenbury	03 16 00	
	of Benjamine Whittenbury	00 05 00	
Oct 2	Recd of Thomas Adams of Welches	02 00 00	
	Recd of William Pennyfather	05 10 00	
Oct 26	Recd of Joseph Hudson	01 10 00	
26	Recd of William Ives	05 05 00	
	Recd of Daniell Crawley for Small Tythes	02 00 00	
	Recd of John Freelove	01 05 00	
28	Recd of John Pearse senr	01 12 00	
	of Daniel Adams for Woods	00 06 00	
	of Daniel Crawley for Small Tythes	02 00 00	
XXX[81]	of Thomas Halse [82] Esq for Offerings for 2 Years	01 01 00	
Nov 7	Recd of William Butterfield	08 10 00	
8	Recd of William Game	04 10 00	
15	Recd of William Emmins in full	06 00 00	
	Recd of Thomas French in part	01 05 00	
16	Received of George Acher for Wid[o]w Whittenberry	00 16 00	
	Received of Thomas Venables	00 06 00	
20	Received of John Miller	00 10 00	
	Received of Joseph Webster	00 15 00	
	Received of Nathaniel Asser	02 10 00	
	Received of John Smith at the White House	01 02 00	
	Recd of John Smith the short	00 01 06	
Dec 2	Recd of William Wallis for Small Tythes	01 15 00	
5	Recd of John Goose for Small Tythes	02 00 00	

[81] There is no indication as to what these crosses mean
[82] This is the only mention of Thomas Halse. Three of his children were baptised at Datchworth including Frances on 12 August 1725 who died a year later and was buried in the nave of Datchworth church (HALS: DP/33/1/2). This offering may have been associated with this event. There is no known connection with the Halsey family of Great Gaddesdon

Recd of [*blank*] Titmasse for Small Tythes	00	06 00
Recd of Edward Pennyfather	00	07 00
Recieved of John Field 'by Wood'	05	05 00
Received of William Blindall	11	00 00
Received of James Whitehall	20	00 00
Received of John Pearse junr	01	00 00
Received of Mr John Haynes	00	10 00
Received of Thomas Kimpton	12	06 00
Recd of Joseph Baldock	00	02 00

[*Total excluding entry for Daniel Crawley above*] [*105 06 06*]

[46] Tythes due at Harvest & Michaelmasse 1729

1729

Sep 30	Received of Thomas Miller in full	00	10 00
30	Received of James Whitehall in part	10	00 00
Oct 3	Received of William Whittenbury	03	16 00
6	Received of George Acher	00	16 00
25	Received of William Pennyfather	05	10 00
	Thomas Adams of Welches	02	00 00
	John Pearse senr	01	12 00
	of Mr Daniel Adams for Woods	00	06 00
	Widowe Culver	00	03 00
Nov 13	Received of William Emmins	06	00 00
11	Received of William Ives	05	05 00
18	Received of John Smith of the White House	01	02 00
26	Received of William Wallis for Small Tythes	01	10 00
29	Received of Daniel Mardell	00	02 06
Dec 4	Received of Thomas Kimpton	12	06 00
	Received of William Game	06	10 00
4	Received of William Butterfield	07	10 00
	Received of John Goose for Small Tythes	02	00 00
	Received of John Freelove	01	05 00

Received of James Whitehall in full	10	0	00
Received of Joseph Webster	00	10	00
Received of Nathaniel Asser	02	10	00
Recd of John Venables	01	08	00
Recd of John French	[blank]		
Recd of Thomas Nash of Bragher End for Small Tythes	00	07	06
Recd of John Titmasse for Small Tythes	00	06	00
Recd of Robert King Esq for Small Tythes	00	10	06
Recd of Christopher Draper for Small Tythes	00	10	00
Recd of Mr Daniel Haynes	00	10	00
Recd of Joseph Hudson	01	10	00
Recd of John Field	05	05	00
Recd of Joseph Baldock	00	02	00
[Total]	[91	12	06]

[47] Receipts of Tythes due at Michaelmasse 1730

Oct	5	Received of William Whittenbury	03	15	00
	9	Received of Elizabeth Crawley for her small Tythes as usual	02	00	00
		For Tythe of Turnips sold that Year	02	00	00
	11	Received of William Pennyfather	05	10	00
	11	Received of Thomas Adams of Welches	02	00	00
	11	Received of James Whitehall in part	10	00	00
	11	Received of William Wallis for small Tythes as usual	01	15	00
	11	Recd of him for Tythe if Turnips sold that Year	01	05	00
	11	Received of William Deards	02	05	00
	19	Recd of John Smith the Short for two Years	00	03	00
	20	Received of Joseph Hudson	01	10	00
	20	Received of John Smith the Long	01	02	00
	25	Recd of William Emmins	06	00	00
	27	Recd of John Pearse senr	01	13	00

27	Recd of Daniel Adams for Woods	00	06	00
	Received of James Whitehall more in full	10	00	00
	Received of William Butterfield	07	10	00

[1730/1]

Jan 15	Received of John Field	05	05	00
	Received of William Game	07	00	00
	Received of the Widowe Ives	05	05	00
	Received of Thomas Kimpton	12	06	00
	Received of John Pearse junr	01	00	00
	Received of Mr Daniel Hayne	00	10	00
	Received of John Phipp	01	*[blank]*	
	Received of William Blindall by Rent of Barnes	11	10	00
	Received of Joseph Webster	00	16	00
	Received of Christopher Draper for small Tythes	00	10	00
	Received of John Titmasse for small Tythes	00	06	00
	Received of Thomas Nash of Bragher End	00	07	06
	Recd of Edward Mardell of Woolmore Green	00	06	00
	Recd of George Ray	00	03	00
	Recd of the Widowe Culver by the Road	00	03	00
	Received of Edward Pennyfather	00	07	06
	Recd of John Venables	01	04	00
	Recd of Thomas Venables	00	06	00
	[Total]	*[106*	*19*	*00]*

[48] Receipts of Tythes due at Michaelmasse 1730

[1730/1]

[Jan 15]	Received of Nathaniel Asser	02	10	00
	Received of Crawley of Burnham Green	00	06	00
	Received of Rowland Mardell by acct	00	10	00
	Received of Joseph Baldock	00	02	00
	Received of John Freelove	01	05	00
	Received of Daniel Mardell	00	02	06

[*illeg*]	Received of Joseph Clarke Esq	04 00 00
	Received of George Acher	00 16 00
	Received of Benjamine Uncle	00 05 00
		[*Total*] [*09 16 06*]

[49] Receipts of Tythes etc due at Midsummer and Michaelmasse 1731

Jul	Received of Benjamin Uncle for an Acre of seed Turnips[83]	05 05 00
Jul	X Received of Joseph Clarke Esq for Tythes of Bragher End Meadows & Garden X [84]	04 00 00
Oct 1	Recieved of James Whitehall in part	10 00 00
Oct 14	of Edward Pennyfather of Harmer Green	05 10 00
	Recd of Thomas Adams of Welches	02 00 00
Oct 26	Recd of John Pearse senr	01 12 00
	Recd of him for Mr Adam's Woods	00 06 00
Nov 1	Recd of William Whittenbury	03 15 00
Nov 8	Received of John Freelove	01 04 00
8	Received of John Pearse junr	01 00 00
Nov 12	Recd of John Bassett senr	00 05 00
	Recd of Elizabeth Crawley Widowe for her Small Tythes as Usual	02 00 00
	For the \Tythe/ of her Turnips sold	00 15 00
	Recd of William Wallis for Small Tythes	01 15 00
Dec 4	Recd of John Smith at the White House	01 02 00
Dec	Received of John Phipp	01 00 00
Dec 24	Received of John Field	05 05 00
	Received of William Blindall of Codicott for the Tythe of Seven Acres of Turnips growing in Feague Shotts[85]	00 14 00
Dec 27	Received of Isaac Turner for 3 Years	00 06 00

---

[83] A substantial tithe for a highly valued commodity
[84] There is no indication as to the meaning of the crosses
[85] Figg Shot on the 1839 tithe map (HALS: DSA4/34/2)

[?28]	Recieved of James Whitehall more in full	10	0	00
	Received of Joseph Hudson	01	10	00

[1731/2]

Jan	1	Received of George Acher	00	16	00
	3	Received of Edd Pennyfather senr	00	07	00
		Received of John Venables for North's Land	00	15	00
		Received of John Crawley of Burnham Green	00	06	00
	5	Received of Joseph Webster of West End	00	15	00
	7	Received of Nathaniel Asser	02	10	00
		Received of Christopher Draper for Small Tythes	00	10	00
	10	Received of Thomas Kimpton	12	06	00
		Received of Thomas Nash of Bragher End for Small Tythes	00	07	06
		Received of Mr Daniel Haynes	00	10	00
		Received of Christopher Draper for Small Tythes	00	10	00
		[*£78 16 6d*]	79	06	06

[50] 1731 *Receipts of tithes continued*

[1731/2]

Jan	31	Received of John Miller	00	10	00
Feb	4	Received of John Titmasse for small Tythes	00	06	00
		Recd of Thomas Hill	00	02	00
Jan	24	Recd of William Butterfield	07	10	00
Jan	27	Recd of Daniel Mardell by his Wife	00	02	06
1732					
Jun	11	Recieved of Pallatt	00	12	00
Jun	18	Recd of Joseph Baldock	00	02	00
1733					
Oct	9	Recd of John Bassett junr for his Orchard	00	06	00
1733					
Nov	2	Recd of Benjamine Uncle	00	05	00
		[*Total*]	[*09*	*15*	*06*]

TITHE ACCOUNTS

[51] Receipts of Tythes dues at Midsummer & Michalmasse 1732

Jun	24	Received of Joseph Clarke Esq	04	00	00
Sep	29	Received of Mr Daniel Hayne	00	10	00
Oct	3	Recd of James Whitehall in part	10	00	00
	3	Recd of Elizabeth Crawley for her own Small Tythes	02	00	00
		of Ditto for 10 Acres of Turnips sold	01	00	00
		of Ditto for Rent of Piece of Glebe Land in Rush Mead	00	02	00
	5	Recd of William Whittenberry	03	15	00
	6	Recd of Thomas Adams of Welches	02	00	00
		Recd of Edward Pennyfather	05	10	00
	17	Recd of John Pearse senr	01	12	00
		of Mr Daniel Adams for Woods	00	06	00
	19	Recd of Robert Adams in part	02	05	00
	31	Recd of William Game	08	06	00
Nov	5	Received of John Field in part 4:4:0 \ in part/in full[86]	05	05	00
	20	Recd of William Wallis for his own Small Tythes	01	15	00
		for 7 Acres of Turnips at 2 sh per Acre	00	14	00
Jan	1	Thomas Venables Recd of him	00	06	00
	2	Edward Pennyfather recd of him	00	07	00
	12	Recd of James Whitehall in full	10	00	00
	13	Received of George Acher	00	16	00
	15	Recd of John Venables	00	18	00
		Recd of [blank] Pallett	00	10	00
	16	Recd of Robert Adams more in full	01	09	00
	18	Recd of Joseph Webster	00	15	00
	29	Recd of John Titmasse for Small Tythes	00	06	00
Feb	5	Received of Thomas Hills	00	02	00
	5	Received of William Deards senr	02	05	00
Mar	26	Received of Thomas Kimpton	21	00	00
1733					

---

[86] 'in part' and 'in full' appear to have been added later

Oct	9	Received of John Bassett junr	00	13 00
Nov	2	Received of Benjamine Uncle	00	05 00
			[*Total*] [*88*	*12 00*]

[52] Receipts for Tythes due at Midsummer & Michaelmasse 1733

Oct	1	Recd of William Wallis for Small Tythes	01	15 00
		For Turnips which he sold last Winter 8 Acres	00	16 00
Oct	3	Received of James Whitehall in part	10	00 00
	8	Received of Robert Adams in part	02	10 00
		Received of Elizabeth Crawley Widowe for Small Tythes	02	00 00
		For 10 Acres of Turnips sold last Winter	01	00 00
		For 1 Years Rent of the Piece of Glebe Land in Rush Mead [87]	00	02 00
		Received of Edward Pennyfather	05	10 00
	9	Recd of John Bassett junr	00	13 00
		Recd of Thomas Adams of Welches	02	00 00
	27	Recd of William Game in full	08	06 00
	30	Recd of William Whittenberry	03	15 00
	31	Received of John Pearse senr	01	12 00
Nov	2	Received of Benjamin Uncle	00	05 00
		Recd of Mr Daniel Adams for Woods	00	06 00
		Recd of William Deards	02	00 00
	12	Recd of William Butterfield	07	00 00
	19	Recd of Thomas Kimpton in part	10	00 00
	26	Recd of Joseph Hudson	01	10 00
Dec	24	Recd of Edward Pennyfather	00	06 00
		Recd of George Acher	00	16 00
[1733/4]				
Jan	5	Recd of Robert Adams more in full	01	04 00
	5	Recd of Thomas Venables	00	06 00

---

[87] Little Rush Mead (55 on 1839 tithe map) is next to a piece of glebe. See also Figure 4

	9	Recd of John Goose for his own Small Tythes	02 00 00
		For the Tythe of Turnips sold for ten pounds	01 00 00
		Recd of Thomas Jeaques junr for his Small Tythes	00 02 06
		Recd of Joseph Webster	00 15 00
		Recd of John Titmasse for Small Tythes	00 06 00
Feb	4	Recd of Edward Mardell of Woolmore Green	00 06 00
		Recd of Nathaniell Asser	02 10 00
	26	Recd of Thomas Kimpton in full	11 00 00
			[Total] [81 11 06]

[53] Receipts for Tythes due at Michaelmasse 1734

Oct	9	Received of William Whittenborough	03 15 00
	10	Recd of James Whitehall in part	10 00 00
	11	Recd of Elizabeth Crawley for her Small Tythes	02 00 00
		for [blank] Acres of Turnips sold at 2sh per Acre	[blank]
		for Rent of piece of Glebe in Rush Mead	00 02 00
	12	Recd of William Game in full	08 10 00
	14	Recd of William Wallis for Small Tythes	01 15 00
		said he sold No Turnips	[blank]
	17	Recd of John Pearse senr	01 12 00
	19	Recd of long John Smith for the Whitehouse	01 02 00
	19	Recd of Thomas Adams of Welches	02 00 00
	19	Recd of Edward Pennyfather	05 10 00
		Recd of Thomas Venables	00 06 00
		Recd of John Godfrey	01 00 00
		Recd of Joseph Hudson	01 12 00
	28	Recd of short John Smith	00 01 06
	28	Recd of Benjamin Whittenbury	00 05 00
Dec	10	Recd of Joseph Webster	00 15 00
[1734/5]			
Jan	6	Recd of James Whitehall more in full	10 00 00
		Recd of John Field	05 05 00

Recd of William Butterfield	07 00 00
Recd of Thomas Kimpton in part	16 10 00
Recd of Mr Daniel Hayne	00 10 00
Recd of George Acher	00 16 00
Recd of John Venables	00 18 00
Recd of Nathaniel Asser by a Cowe	02 10 00
Recd of John Pearse junr[88]	01 [blank]
Recd of Daniel Mardell	00 02 06
Received of [blank] Pallett	00 12 00
Received of Thomas Venables	00 06 00
	[Total] [85 15 00]

[54] Receipts of Tythes due at Michaelmasse etc 1735

Oct	27	Received of John Pearse senr for his own	01 12 00
		of him for Mr Adams's Woods	00 06 00
	28	Recd of William Whittenberry	03 15 00
	28	Recd of James Whitehall in part	10 00 00
	28	of Mr Haynes	00 10 00
		Recd of Thomas Adams of Welches by John Bassett	02 00 00
		of William Pennyfather by Ditto	05 10 00
	28	Recd of John Crawley for his small Tythes	02 00 00
		for the Tythe of 5 Acres of Turnips sold	00 07 06
		for the Rent of a piece of Glebe Land in Mr King's Rush Mead	00 02 00
	29	Recd of Thomas Kimpton in part	10 10 00
Nov	15	Received of William Game in full	08 10 00
	17	Received of John Smith of the White House	01 00 00
		Received of John Godfrey	01 00 00
		Received of John Field	05 05 00
	18	Received of William Blindall	03 03 00
		Received of William Wallis upon acct	01 15 00

---

[88] It has been assumed that John Pearse junior paid £1 as he did in 1731, [49]

60

	Recd of John Goose for small Tythes	02	00	00
	for Turnips sold	00	06	00
Dec 20	Recd of William Butterfield in part	07	00	00
1736[89]				
Mar 7	Recd of Daniel Mardell for small Tythes	00	02	06
	Received of John Pearse junr[90]	01	*[blank]*	
	Receivd of George Acher	00	16	00
	Recd of John Venables	00	18	00
	Recd of *[blank]* Pallett	00	12	00
	Recd of Thomas Venables	00	06	00
1738				
May 2	Received of Benjamine Whittenberry	00	05	00
	[Total]	*[70*	*11*	*00]*

[55] Receipts at Datchworth due at Midsummer & Michaelmasse 1736

Oct 18	Received of John Pearse senr for his own Tythes	01	12	00
	Received of him before for Mr Adams's Woods	00	06	00
Oct 19	Received of Mr Daniel Hayne	00	15	00
Oct 28	Received of Robert Adams in full	04	14	00
	Received of George Acher	00	16	00
29	Received of John Crawley for his Small Tythes	02	00	00
	of him for Turnips sold 6 Acres for 7 pds	00	14	00
	of him \for/ Rent of a piece of Glebe in Rush Mead	00	02	00
	Received of James Whitehall in part	10	00	00
Nov 15	Received of Thomas Kimpton in full	21	00	00
	Received of William Game in full	08	16	00
Nov 18	Received of William Blindall in full	03	03	00
25	Received of John Godfrey in full	01	00	00
26	Received of John Smith of the White house	01	02	00

---

[89] This may be 1735/6 or 1736/7. It is possible that Hawtayne is using the 'new' year as it is so close to March 25. See similar entry [55]

[90] It has been assumed that John Pearse junior's amount is £1 as before, [53]

[?26]	Received of William Butterfield in full	07	00	00
Dec 11	Received of John Field in full	05	05	00
Dec 25	Received of Edward Pennyfather Senr	00	07	00
	Received of John Venables	00	06	00
28	Received of James Whitehall in full	10	00	00
29	Recd of John Lowen & Robert Heath for Ginns	00	06	00
	Recd of Joseph Webster at West End	00	16	00
	Recd of Peter Crawley for the Gun	01	05	00
	Received before in Novr of William Pennyfather junr	05	10	00
	of Thomas Adams of Welches	02	00	00
	of Fawlkener	02	12	00
	of Christopher Draper	00	15	00
	of Joseph Hudson	01	12	00
	of William Whittenberry	03	10	00
1737[91]				
Mar 7	Received of John Titmasse for Small Tythes	00	06	00
	Received of Daniel Mardell for Small Tythes	00	02	06
Oct 11	Recd of John Bassett senr	00	10	00
1738				
May 2	Received of Benjamine Whittenberry	00	05	00
1738/9				
Jan 10	Recd of Thomas Hills	00	02	00
	Recd of Edward Mardell of Woolmore Green	00	06	00
		[Total]	*[98*	*15*	*06]*

[56] Receipts at Datchworth due at Midsummer & Michaelmasse [1737]

Oct 4	Received of Robert Adams for 27 Acres of Land	02	14	00
	Received of George Acher for Small Tythes	00	07	00
	Received of William Whittenberry	03	15	00
5	Received of Edward Pennyfather	00	07	00

---

[91] See [54] footnote

	5	Received of William Pennyfather	05	10	00
	8	Received of Thomas Adams of Welches	02	00	00
	8	Long John Smith of the White house	01	02	00
	10	William Wallis for Small Tythes	01	15	00
		John Godfrey	01	00	00
		James Whitehall for Small Tythes	02	02	00
		John Goose for Small Tythes	02	00	00
		For the Tythe of 5 Acres of Turnips sold	00	10	00
	11	Received of John Bassett junr	03	03	00
	15	Received of John Crawley for Small Tythes	02	00	00
		for ten acres of Turnips sold at 1: 10: 0 pr Acre[92]	01	01	00
		for Rent of piece of Glebe in Rush Mead	00	02	00
		Recd of Thomas Nash of Bragher End	00	07	00
Oct	17	Recd of John Pearse Senr	01	12	00
		of Joseph Hudson	01	10	00
Dec	3	Received of [blank] Falkener by Old Titmasse	02	10	00
	7	Recd of John Field in full	05	07	06
	17	Recd of William Game	08	10	00
		Recd of Peter Crawley	01	06	00
		of Joseph Webster	00	16	00
		of John Venables	00	06	00
		of William Butterfield for Small Tythes	01	00	00

[1737/8]

Feb	27	Recd of John Titmasse for Small Tythes	00	06	00

1738

May	2	Received of Benjamine Whittenberry	00	05	00

[1738/9]

Jan	10	Received of Thomas Hills	00	02	00
	11	Recd of Edward Mardell of Woolmore Green	00	06	00

1739

---

[92] The tithe entry should be £1 10s

TITHE ACCOUNTS

Jun	13	Received of Thomas Kimpton for Small Tythes	02	15	00
		of Elizabeth Pierce Widowe	01	04	00
		of Thomas Jeaques	00	05	00
		of [blank] Pallett	00	12	00
		[Total]	[58	07	06]

[57] Receipts of Tythes due in the Year 1738

Oct	4	Received of Mr Daniel Haines	00	15	00
	14	Recd of Edward Pennyfather senr	00	07	00
	14	Recd of Thomas Adams of Welches	02	00	00
	16	Recd of Edward Pennyfather junr of Harmer Green	05	10	00
	16	Recd of John Godfrey for great Tythes	01	00	00
	16	Received of William Whittenbury	03	15	00
	16	Received of John Crawley for small Tythes	02	00	00
		for piece of Glebe in Rush Mead	00	02	00
	16	Received of John Goose for small Tythes	02	00	00
	21	Received of William Wallis for small Tythes	01	15	00
	24	Received of John Pearse senr	01	12	00
	27	Received of James Whitehall for Small Tythes	02	00	00
		Received of William Game	08	10	00
		Received of Joseph Hudson	01	12	00
~~Nov~~	~~6~~				
Nov	28	Received of William Blindall	03	03	00
[1738/9]					
Jan	6	Received of John Venables	01	02	00
		Thomas Venables	00	06	00
		Long John Smith	01	02	00
		Peter Crawley	01	06	00
Jan	9	of John Field	05	05	00
	10	of Thomas Hills	00	02	00
	11	of Edward Mardell of Woolmore Green	00	06	00
Feb	16	of Joseph Webster	00	16	00

28	Received of Thomas Nash of Bragher End	00 07 06	
	of Faulkener	02 12 00	
	Received of Elizabeth Pearse Widowe	01 04 00	
	~~Mr Danl Haynes~~	*[blank]*	

[1739]

Jun	13	Recieved of Thomas Kimpton for small Tythes	02 15 00
		Received of Thomas Jeaques for all Tythes	00 08 00

[Total] *[53 12 06]*

[58] Payments of Tythes due upon the Harvest 1740[93]

Sep		Recd of Thomas Adams of Welches in full	02 00 00
Sep		Received of James Whitehall in part	10 00 00
Oct	8	Received of William Pennyfather in full	05 10 00
Ditto		of John Goose in part	04 00 00
Ditto		of William Wallis in part	04 00 00
Oct	17	Recd of John Pearse in full	01 12 00
Oct	18	Recd of John Smith of the White house	01 02 00
Nov	4	Received of John Whittenberry in full	03 15 00
		Received of Richard Falkner in full	02 10 00
		Recd of Joseph Hudson in full	01 10 00
		Received of Daniel Mardell	00 02 06
Nov	14	Received of Christopher Wade in part for 20 Years	00 05 00
	15	Received of Robert Mardell for 4 Years	00 02 08
		Received more of John Goose upon Acct	05 10 00
		Recd of John Hewson for 2 Years	00 01 04
		Received of Thomas Threader of Sheephall for 2 Years	00 12 00
		Received of William Game in full	09 00 00
		Received of William Butterfield in full	03 14 00
		Received of John Godfrey in full	01 02 00
		Received of Edward Pennyfather in full for 2 Years	00 14 00

---

[93] There is a blank untitled page between years 1738 and 1740

		Received of Benjamine Uncle for 2 Years	00	10	00
Dec	17	Received of Thomas Nash of Bragher End for 2 Years	01	00	00
		Received of William Blindall	03	03	00
		Received of John Titmasse upon Acct	00	18	00
Dec	2	Received of James Whitehall in full	10	00	00
Dec	2	Received of John Field in full	05	05	00
Dec	17	Received of William Wallis more in full	05	10	00
1741					
Sep	15	Received of Robert Adams in full	02	10	00
1742/3					
Jan	1	Received of John Bassett senr for a Year[94]	00	05	00
		[*Total*]	[*86*	*03*	*06*]

[59] Receipts for Tythes 1741

Sep	14	Received of John Whittenberry in full	03	15	00
	15	Received of Robert Adams in full	02	10	00
Oct	17	Received of [*blank*] Pennyfather in full	05	10	00
		Recd of Edward Prior in full	02	05	00
		of Peter Crawley	01	06	00
		of ~~Edward~~ Joseph Webster	00	16	00
		of [*blank*]Faulkener	02	12	00
Oct	26	Received of James Whitehall	20	00	00
		of Thomas Kimpton	20	00	00
		of William Wallis	09	10	00
		of John Goose	09	10	00
		of John Godfrey	01	00	00
		of William Butterfield	03	14	00
		of Joseph Hudson	01	10	00
		of John Pearse senr	01	12	00

---

[94] This entry is repeated on [59] and [60] possibly suggesting another example of back payments

	of John Smith at the White house	01	02	00
	of William Blindall	03	03	00
	of John Bassett junr	03	00	00
Oct 31	Received of John Venables	01	00	00
Nov 9	Received of John Crawley	16	00	00
11	of Phipp by his Bill	01	05	00
[1741/2]				
Jan 6	Received of Thomas Jeaques	00	08	00
9	Received of Thomas Venables	00	06	00
	Received of [*blank*] Titmasse by the Common	01	01	00
13	Received of Edward Mardell for Tythe Turnips 3 Acres	00	06	00
1742/3				
Jan 1	Received of John Bassett senr for a Year	00	05	00
Jan 3	Received of Francis Kimpton for a Year	00	04	00
	[*Total*]	[*113*	*10*	*00*]

[60] Receipts of Tythes from Michaelmasse 1741 to Michaelmasse 1742
[1742]

Oct 1	Received of John Whittenberry at twice for the Year	04	10	00
15	Received of Joseph Stevenson at twice	06	06	00
	and a Fatt Goose	00	03	06
15	Recd of Edward Pennyfather senr	00	07	00
	Recd of Edward Pennyfather junr	05	10	00
	Recd of Mrs Reeves for small Tythes	00	05	00
	Received of Thomas Neots in full at twice	04	10	00
	Received of Robert Adams for small Tythes & Turnips	00	19	00
16	Received of William Blindall for small Tythes & Turnips	00	18	08
	Received of John Godfrey in full	01	00	00
23	Received of Peter Crawley in full	01	10	00
25	Received of John Smith	01	02	00

	Received of John Bassett junr	03	[blank]	
	Received of Mrs Reeves for her Cow	00	05	00
Nov 1	Received of John Pearse in full	02	00	00
	Edward Mardell junr	02	00	00
Nov 10	Received of James Whitehall for the Berry	20	00	00
30	Received of John Phipp	01	10	00
Dec 11	Received of Thomas Goose for small Tythes	02	00	00
Dec 13	Received of John Venables	01	00	00
15	Received of Thomas Venables	00	07	06
	Received of John Miller	00	12	06
	Received of Edward Mardell senr	00	06	00
16	Received of John Titmasse for small Tythes	00	07	06
	Received of Thomas Jeaques in part	00	08	00
1742/3				
Jan 1	Received of John Bassett senr for oneYear	00	05	00
14	Received of [blank] Faircloath for Joseph Hudsons small Tythes	00	10	00
1743				
Mar 25	Received of William Butterfield for the Dell Close	00	01	00
	[Total]	[61	13	08]

[61] Receipts for Tythes from Michaelmasse 1742 to Ditto 1743

1743

Sep [?4]	Received of James Whitehall in part[95]	10	00	00
Oct 17	Received of ~~William~~ Edward Pennyfather in full	05	10	00
	Received of [blank] Fletcher in full	02	00	00
	Received of John Godfrey in full	01	00	00
	Received of Edward Prior of Dardes End in full	02	15	00
	Received of Thomas Kimpton in part	10	10	00
	Received of John Crawley in part	10	00	00
	Received of William Game in part	05	05	00

---

[95] The date is doubtful because the '4' is preceded by an ink blob

	Received of John Miller	00	12	06
24	Received of John Whittenberry	04	10	00
30	Recd of John Smith by a Red Cow	01	02	00
	Recd of George Acher	02	00	00
Nov 14	Recd of Edward Mardell junr	02	00	00
16	Received of Thomas Goose for small Tythes	02	00	00
17	Received of William Wallis for small Tythes	02	00	00
18	Received of John Bassett senr for his Tythes	00	05	00
18	Recieved of John Crawley more upon Acct	06	00	00
19	Received of John Pearse senr in full	02	00	00
19	Received more of Hudson for James Whitehall	05	05	00
19	Received ~~more~~ of Peter Crawley in full	01	10	00
Dec 27	Received of Jane Whitehall Widowe in full[96]	04	15	00
	Received of Charles Philpott for a Year	00	07	06
	Received of Edward Pennyfather senr	00	07	06

1743/4

Jan 2	Received of Thomas Adams of Welches for small Tythes	00	12	06
2	Recd of Thomas Venables in full	00	07	06
3	Received more of Thomas Kimpton in part	08	08	00
	Received of William Blindall for small Tythes	00	14	00
	Received of Robert Adams for small Tythes	00	11	00
4	Received of Thomas Threader \of Sheephall/ for the Tythe of three acres in Catchpole	00	06	00
	Received of Thomas Jeaques in full for all Tythes	00	08	00
	Received of John Titmasse for small Tythes	00	07	06
	Received more of Thomas Kimpton in full	01	02	00

1744

Apr 26	Received of John Cater for his Garden	00	05	00

---

[96] The entry in the £ column is not clear. It is assumed that it is £4 thus making a total of £20 which is what Whitehall paid in 1742 **[60]**. He probably died after he had paid his first instalment of £10. He died in 1743, aged 76 (HALS: DP/33/1/2)

	Received of John Venables for all Tythes	01	00	00
May 25	Received of Joseph Stephenson in full	06	06	00
	[Total]	[102	02	00]

[62] Receipts for Tythes from Michsse 1743 to Michsse 1744[97]

1744				
Received of James Whitehalls Exectrs for the Berry	20	00	00
Received of Edward Pennyfather of Harmer Green	05	10	00
of [blank]Fletcher at Datchworth Green	02	00	00
of John Godfrey for the Mote house	01	00	00
of Edward Prior of Deardes End	02	15	00
and a Dozn of Pidgeons ['Prior' in margin]	[blank]		
of Thomas Kimpton of Swangleys	21	00	00
of John Crawley of Bragher End	16	00	00
of William Game of Raffing Green Farme	09	00	00
of John Whittenberry	04	10	00
of John Miller	00	12	06
of John Smith of Bulls Green	01	02	00
of George Acher	02	00	00
of Edward Mardell junr	02	00	00
of Thomas Goose for small Tythes	02	00	00
of William Wallis for small Tythes	02	00	00
of John Pearse	02	00	00
of Thomas Nash of Bragher End	00	12	06
of Peter Crawley in full	01	10	00
of Charles Phillpott	00	07	06
of Edward Pennyfather senr	00	07	06
of Thomas Adams junr of Welches	02	10	00
of Thomas Venables of Bulls Green	00	07	06
of William Blindall for small Tythes	00	14	00
of [blank]Burnage for small Tythes	00	10	00

---

[97] The first column only contained odd notes as shown, but no dates

of Thomas Threader of Sheephall for 3 acres in a
Field called Catchpole dividing between Aston and
Sheephall and Datchworth   00 06 00

of John Titmasse for small Tythes   00 07 06

of Thomas Jeaques in full   00 08 00

of John Cater for his Garden ['Cater' *in margin*]   00 05 00

of John Bassett senr   00 05 00

of John Bassett junr   03 03 00

of Joseph Stephenson   05 10 00

X   of [*blank*]Neots   04 10 00

of Daniel Mardell   00 03 00

of Mr Daniell Haynes for small Tythes   00 10 00

of Francis Kimpton   00 01 00

of [*blank*]Fullfarr   00 08 00

of John Ipgrave   00 01 00

of John Phipp   01 10 00

of John Freelove   00 01 00

[*blank*]Wood   [*blank*]

of Joseph Draper   00 01 06

of Thomas Nash   00 01 00

[*Total*] [*117 19 06*]

[63] Receipts for Tythes for the Year Ending at Michaelmasse 1745

Oct 7	Received of William Fletcher at 2 payments	02 00 00	
Oct 11	Received of Mr Thomas Adams of Welches at twice	02 10 00	
Oct 14	Recd of Thomas Neats at twice[98]	04 02 00	
Oct 30	Recd of Daniel Hayns for small Tythes	00 10 00	
Nov 30	Recd of John Bassett junr	03 00 00	
Nov 20	of Peter Crawley	01 10 00	
	of the Widdow Hudson for small Tythes at the Berry	03 00 00	
	of Thomas Goose for small Tythes	02 00 00	

---

[98] The entries underlined are in a different hand, probably Hawtayne's son

of William Wallis for small Tythes	02 00 00
of Thomas Nash of Bragher End	00 12 06
of John Titmasse for small Tythes	00 07 06
of Thomas Jeaques in full for all Tythes	00 08 00
of John Crawley for his own Tythes	16 00 00
for small Tythes of Mr Kings Meadows	[*blank*]
for rent of piece of Glebe in Rushy Mead	00 02 06
of Benjamine Uncle	00 03 00
of [*blank*]Fulfarr	00 08 00
of John Ipgrave	[*blank*]
of William Blindall for small Tythes	00 10 00
of Thomas Neots	04 10 00
of Daniel Mardell	00 [*blank*]
of Joseph Stephenson in [full?][99] for all Tythes	05 10 00
of George Waughby for small Tythes	00 06 00
of Francis Kimpton	00 01 00
of William Mardell	00 01 00
of Daniel Mardell junr	00 01 00
of Richard Catlin	00 01 00
of William Skegg	00 01 00
of William Fletcher	02 00 00
of John Pearse	02 00 00
of John Godfrey	01 00 00
of John Smith of Bulls Green	01 02 00
of ~~John~~ \Thomas/ Venables ~~of Edward Grey~~	00 07 06
of Edward Grey	00 01 06
of Edward Pennyfather	00 07 06
of John Venables	01 00 00
of William Faulkener for small Tythes	00 13 00

---

[99] The word 'full' has probably been omitted. 'In full' would be consistent with his payments in 1746 and 1747

of S Roe for small Tythes	00 02 06
of Nathaniel Asser for small Tythes	00 00 00
of [*blank*] Pennyfather shoe maker at Burnham Green	00 05 00
of [*blank*] Phipp at Burnham Green	00 01 00
of George Ellis	00 01 00
of Richard Cutt	00 01 00
of Charles Phillpott	00 07 06
for Robert Heaths house Empty for 3 other houses Opposite to it \William Langley and Abraham Nott/	00 03 00
of Mr Adams of Welches	02 10 00
for 2 Houses late Barnetts	00 02 00
[*Total*]	[*61 19 00*]

[64] Receipts for Tythes for the Year Ending Michaelmasse 1745

of John Cater of Govers Green	00 05 00
of William Thorp	00 03 00
of Benjamine Whittenberry	00 05 00
of Joseph Draper	00 01 06
of [*blank*]Waple	00 01 00
of [*blank*]	00 01 00
of John Frelove	00 01 00
of Isaac Turner	00 01 06
of Thomas Ipgrave[100]	00 01 00
of Mr Daniel Haynes for small Tythes	00 10 00
of John Bassett senr	00 05 00
of Thomas Turner	00 02 00
of Israil Chalkely	00 01 00
of Christophr Wade	00 01 00
of Daniel Brooks	00 01 00
of John Worledge	00 00 06
of Thomas Nash of Raffin Green	00 01 00

---

[100] John has been overwritten Thos

of [*blank*]Ipgrave at the Church House	00	01	00
of Richard Ansell	00	01	00
of George Harding	00	00	06
of John Brograve	00	01	00
of George Nash	00	02	00
of Thomas Clarke ~~of the~~	00	02	00
of the Widowe Ives for her Orchard etc	00	02	00
of [*blank*]Burnage for small Tythes	00	10	00
of George Ray	00	03	00
of Edward Mardell for Hawkins's Land	02	00	00
of George Acher	02	00	00
of the Widowe Mardell of Woolmore Green	00	06	00
of John Whittenberry	04	10	00
of John Phipp shoemaker	01	10	00
of Thomas Kimpton for Swangleys small Tythes	02	00	00
of Edward Prior of Deards End	02	15	00
of John Miller of West End	00	12	06
of Peter Crawley	01	10	00
of the Widowe Webster for small Tythes	00	04	00
of Thomas Smith of Mardley Berry for 3 acres of Land of the Widowe Mardlins at Welling	00	07	06
of Thomas Kimpton for the great Tythes of Swangleys and other Lands	18	00	00
William Game for Raffin Green Farme	09	00	00
of Richard Blindall for Col[t]sfoot Farme	11	10	00
The Tythe of Barnes Closes in hand[101]	03	02	06
~~Abram Nott and William Langley of BurnhamGreen~~	~~00~~	~~03~~	~~00~~
of George Waughby for small Tythes	00	04	00
[*Total*]	[*62*	*15*	*06*]
[*From* **[63]**]	[*61*	*19*	*00*]
[*Grand total for 1745*]	[*124*	*14*	*06*]

---

[101] The £ entry is not clear but £3 has been assumed because **[65]** also records 'Tythe of Barnes Closes' £3 2s 6d

[65] Receipts for Tythes Ending at Michaelmasse 1746

Sep	30	Received of John Godfrey in full	01	00	00
Oct	15	Received of John Whittenberry at 2 payments	04	10	00
Oct	16	of John Phipp	01	10	00
Oct	29	of Joseph Stephenson in full 2 payments	05	10	00
	31	of William Fletcher at 2 payments in full	02	00	00
Nov	3	of William Game at 2 payments in full	09	00	00
	4	of Edward Pennyfather at Bulls Green in full	00	08	00
		of Mrs Adams of Welches	02	10	00
	8	of Peter Crawley in full	01	10	00
		of Thomas Nash of Bragher End	00	12	06
	15	of Edward Mardell of Woolmore Green	02	00	00
	15	of Edward Prior of Dardes End	02	15	00
	24	of John Pearse at 2 payments	02	00	00
		of William Wallis at 2 payments for small Tythes	02	00	00
	26	of Edward Pennyfather of Harmer Green 3 paymts	05	10	00
		of Thomas Neots of Hawkins Hall 2 paymnts	04	00	00
Dec	28	of John Venables	01	00	00
		of Thomas Venables	00	07	06
		of [blank] Miller at West End	00	12	06

[1746/7]

Jan	15	Received of John Crawley for his Farme and his own land	16	00	00
		of him for Latermarth of Mr King Meads	00	10	00
		for the Rent of a piece of Glebe	00	02	06
	17	Received of Francis Thorpe by a Turkey	00	02	06
		Recd of George \Acher/ at twice	02	00	00
Feb	2	Received of Thomas Jeaques	00	08	00
		Received of John Titmasse for small Tythes	00	06	00
		Received of [blank] Mardle at Bragher End	00	[blank]	
Mar	15	Received of John Smith junr at the White house	01	02	00

23	Received of Thomas Fulfarr	00	08	00
	Recd of William Butterfield	00	01	00

[1747]

Apr 17	Recd of William Blindall for small Tythes	00	10	00
	Received of Thomas Kimpton for Swangleys	*[blank]*		
	Received of Richard Blindall for Coltsfoot Farme	11	10	00
Jul 24	Received of Thomas Goose for small Tythes	02	10	00
	of John Eaton for great Tythes	01	17	06
	of George Waughby for small Tythes	00	04	00
	of William Butterfield for his Dell Field	00	01	00
	of William Blindall senr for small Tythes	00	10	06
	For the Tythe of Barnes Closes in hand	03	02	06
	[Total]	*[90*	*01*	*00]*

[66] Memorandum [*Written by Hawtayne's son shortly before Hawtayne died*]

Such persons as keep a Cow pay Yearly	5s for the same
if Ewes & Lambs by the Score	8s [*Added later in different ink*]10s
for Weathers by d[itt]o	5s [*Added later in different ink*] 8s
Cottagers if an Orchard that be good	1s 6d or 2s
other Cottagers	1s & some but six or seven pence

If the Whole Tythes be lett Turnips are not paid for but if the Tythes of a farm be taken in kind & the Turnips be sold they pay for Tythes   2 s ~~in the pound~~ \pr acre/

[67] Receipts of small Tythes Due at Lady Day 1747[102]

Apr 16 ✓ Received of William Fletcher in part of his Tythes	01	00	00
✓ Received of John Robinson Lytton Esq upon Acct of Tythe Turnips growing Swangleys Farme	04	03	00
Oct 1 ✓ Received of Edward Pennyfather in full	05	10	00

---

[102] Hawtayne died January 2nd 1747/8. The entries underlined are those of his son, who may have added the ticks in the left hand column

7 ✓	of John Whittenberry in full	04	10	00
✓	of Mrs Adams of Welches and other small Tythes	00	10	06
Feb 5 ✓	of Thomas Kimpton for small Tythes & great at the Mote House Farme	<u>01</u>	<u>10</u>	<u>00</u>
7 ✓	of William Hudson for small Tythes & Turnips at the Berry	04	00	00
✓	Received more of William Fletcher in full	01	00	00
✓	Received of the Widowe Pearse in full	02	00	00
✓	Received of John Cater	00	05	00
Nov 10 ✓	Received of [*blank*]Stephenson in full for all Tythes	05	10	00
✓	Received of William Game in full for all Tythes	09	00	00
✓	Received of Thomas Neots	04	00	00
Dec 27 ✓	Received of John Crawley for his Tythes at the Farme at Bragher End and his own Land and the Braches being 30 acres X X X X[103]	16	00	00
Dec 22 ✓	Received of George Acher	02	00	00
	Received of John Eaton	01	17	06
✓	Received of the Widowe Webster	01	00	00
✓	Received of Peter Crawley	01	15	00
✓	Received of [*blank*]Miller	00	12	06
Dec 23 ✓	Received of Edward Pennyfather senr	00	08	06
✓	Received of Thomas Nash of Bragher End	00	13	00
	Received of John Phipp	01	10	00
✓	Received of William Wallis for his own small Tythes in part he haveing for 2 Years past sold several Parcells of Turnips to his son Wallis of Lilly	02	00	00
~~Widow~~ ✓	Received of ~~Edd~~ Mardell ~~widow~~	~~00~~	~~06~~	~~00~~
		00	06	00
✓	of John Crawley for Rent of a Piece of Glebe in Rush Mead part Mr Kings Estate	00	02	00
✓	Received of [*blank*]Mardell of Bragher End	00	03	00

---

[103] Crosses entered by the Rector. Meaning is not known. 'Braches' may be Breeches fields 67, 74 and 75 on the 1839 Datchworth tithe map (HALS: DSA4/34/2)

✓	Received of Benjamine Uncle		00	03 00
	Received of Thomas Fulfarr		00	<u>08</u> 00
✓	Received of Thomas Venables		00	07 06
✓	Received of John Venables		01	00 00
✓	Received of John Smith at the White house		<u>01</u>	02 00
✓	Received of Edward Grey	<u>pd my father</u>	00	02 00
✓	Received of John Cater		[blank]	
✓	Received of Benjamine Whittenberry	<u>pd my father</u>	00	05 00
✓	Recd of [blank]Thorp	<u>d[itt]o</u>	<u>00</u>	<u>02 06</u>
	Thomas Goose		[blank]	
	John Robinson Lytton Esqr		[blank]	
Feb 4	of Mr Game for Tythe of Wood		<u>00</u>	<u>07 00</u>

[Total] [74 17 00]

[68] Inhabitants of the Parish due at Ladyday or Micha\e/lmass[104]

~~Richard Blindall~~	[blank]
Mr King of Brager end	[blank]
William Threader of Sheephall, to my father	00 06 00
William Burri\d/ge[105] small farm, ½ his dues	00 15 00
Richard Faulkne, 26 acres taken in kind[106], to my father	00 10 00
William Blindall Junr, 16 acres taken in kind	[blank]
William Blindall Senr, 32 acres [taken in kind], small Tythes incl. 2 acres Turnips sold & feeding before my Fathers death[107]	00 09 00
John Bassett Senr, 3 yrs Tythes @ 5s; to my Father	00 15 00
John Bassett Junr	[blank]

---

[104] The heading spreads across a double page. This page and [69] are written by Hawtayne's son including notes, sometimes added later in darker ink. There are also occasional ticks and crosses that have been omitted. Although no year is given, it is probably the continuation of the takings for 1747. The new incumbent, Edward Smith, took over on 26 April 1748

[105] Could be Burnage over-written as Burnidge or Burridge

[106] The three entries relating to acres taken in kind are written in the margin

[107] 'feeding' probably means grazing of some description but not necessarily on turnips

TITHE ACCOUNTS

Mr Daniel Haynes		*[blank]*	
Thomas Roe, 2 Yrs at Michaelmass last	00	02	00
Edward Pennyfather, 2s		*[blank]*	
William Pennyfather the Shoemaker, 2 Years	00	08	00
Thomas Jaque, Bill 2s 6d, cash 5s 6d	00	08	00
John Titmass	00	06	00
George Waughby, 2 years	00	08	00
James Adcock	00	03	06
Widow Mardell by the Pond, pd 1s	00	01	00
Charles Philpott		*[blank]*	
William & Robert Mardell Blacksmith, [*illeg*] 2Yrs dues	00	01	04
Isaac Turner, 2s	00	02	00
Thomas Turner, 2s; pd	00	02	00
Thomas Nash, 2[s]	00	02	00
George Nash, 2[s]	00	02	00
John Wood, cottager 1s; pd	00	01	00
Richard Ansell, cott[ager], 1[s]		*[blank]*	
John Hewson, 2s 6[d][108]	00	02	06
John Freelove, cott[ager], 1s 6d; pd 3 years 3s	00	01	06
Joseph Drape, 2s; pd	00	02	00
Widow Ives, cott[ager] 2s		*[blank]*	
	[Total]	*[05*	*07 10]*

[69] Inhabitants *of the Parish*	£	s	d
Ann Roe	00	01	00
Thomas Clarke, 1s	00	01	00
[blank] Waple, 1s	00	01	00
Israel Chalkley, 1s	00	00	08
William Grimes, 1s, now John Wood	00	01	00

---

[108] The position of '2s 6d' on the document is not clear, however it seems more likely to be attached to Hewson than Ansell in the line above

79

TITHE ACCOUNTS

Richard Catlin, 1[s]	00 01 00
George Ellis, 1s	00 01 00
Widow Barnard, 1s	00 01 00
Richard Hewson, 1s	00 01 00
Thomas Ipgrave, 1[s] 0[d]; pd to Easter 1754 Exclusive	00 01 00
John Ipgrave, 1s	00 01 00
William Farr, 1s	[blank]
Christopher Wade, 1s; 2yrs	00 01 00
Daniel Brookes, 1s	[blank]
Jonas Crane, 1s	00 00 08
Thomas Pastell, 1s	00 00 08
John Brograve, 1s [illeg]; nothing	00 00 00
Widow Babb, 1s; house empty	00 01 00
William Ives, 1s	00 01 00
Francis Kimpton, 1[s]	00 02 00
Thomas Phipp, 1[s]	00 00 08
[blank] Shotbolt, 1[s]	00 01 00
George Ray, 2[s]; pd 3s as he told Kimpton the LandL[or]d	00 02 00
[blank] Skegg, 1[s]; [illeg] 2yrs	00 01 00
quere[109], [blank] Langley, 2[s]; now Venables Burnham Green	[blank]
quere, [blank] Nott, 1[s] 6[d]	00 01 06
William Butterfield	[blank]
[blank] Pallett	[blank]
William Hornett	00 00 08
William Catlin	00 01 00
	[Total] [01 04 10]

---

[109] 'quere': probably *quaere*, Latin, meaning to look for or to inquire. Both 'quere' entries were added later with the comment about 'Venables Burnham Green'

[70] *Details of tithes of a few individuals and some agreed amounts in lieu of paying in kind, written by Hawtayne's son.*

		s	
Richard Blindall for small Tythes viz			
5 Cows one Year, he having fed them chiefly out of this Parish	00	12	00
8 Acres Turnips sold at [£]1 1[s] pr Acre[110]	00	16	00
3 Acres d[itt]o	00	03	00
Poors Rates	00	01	06
[*Total*]	01	12	06
George Bennett for 2 yrs to Michaelmass	00	02	00
Mr Prior of Bragerhend for Tythe of 12 Acres Turnips sold at £1 16s pr Acre @ 2s ~~in the pound~~ \pr Acre/	01	04	00
John Crawley for Tythe of 21 Acres Turnips at 2 shills pr Acre	02	02	00
½ the dues for Poors Rates	00	04	00
To be paid in lieu of Tythe Milk & Calf for each Cow yearly	00	05	00
For Ewes in lieu of Tythe Lambs & Wool pr Score	00	10	00
For Weathers Sheep in lieu of Wool & Herbage pr Score	00	08	00
For each Tythe Pigg	00	02	00

[*Several blank pages occur before some miscellaneous entries at the end of the book. The page about haymaking* **[1]** *has been included with the final pages*]

---

[110] Tithe should be approximately 16s 9d. Entry below seems to have used a different rate

TITHE ACCOUNTS

[71] *Reported values of corn in Northumberland and Cumberland, 1739/1740.*

Mr Cook a very serious elderly man and \at/ that time a sergeant in Major Farrers Troop in Earl Cadogans Regiment of Dragoons Quarterd in my Parish of Leighton Bossard in Bedfordshire in the Year 1741. Told me that there [*their*] Regiment being Quarterd in the Countys of Northumberland and Cumberland in the Winter 1739 and the Spring 1740. Told me and was reddy to make Oath of it if desired That

	£	sh	d	
Wheat was sold for	1	4	0	per Bushill
Barley sold at	0	14	6	the Bushill
Oates sold at	0	11	6	the Bushill
Course Bran sold at	0	0	7	the Peck
Hay sold by the stone	0	1	8	14 pds to the stone
Straw sold at a Bundle	0	0	2	of 4 or 5 pds Weight

and he added that He was sure he could have thrust the Bundle into his Boots. In which Winter there was a very hard Frost which began Decr 20[th] 1739 and continued ab[ou]t 2 months Excessively hard

Willm Hawtayne Vicar of Leighton Bossard

[72] *Financial transactions with John Deards, 1735 to 1737.*

An Acct of Goods ~~and moneys~~ sold and delivered and moneys paid to John Deards since the settling of his accts given in to Sept 28 1734 and not reckon'd for in those Bills

1735	In the Spring 1735 John Deards received four calves at			
	1 5 0 each	05	00	00
Jul 14	3 Lambs at 7sh 6d Each	01	02	06
	2 Weather sheep fatt at 15sh Each	01	10	00
	1Ewe at 12sh 6d all these from Sheephall	00	12	06
Aug 21	1 Lamb more at 10sh	00	10	00
Sep 25	2 Porkers at 1 15 0	01	15	00
	In the Winter 2 Q[uarte]rs of White Oates at 16sh	01	02	00
	1 Q[uarte]r & 6 B[ushe]l of Black Oates at	01	04	06
Oct 16	a White Cow	04	04	00
	at the same time paid him \in/ Money	05	05	00
1736	In the Spring 3 Very fine Calves	04	02	06

May 7	3 Lambs 2 Rams & 2 Sheep at	03	00	00
Oct	2 small Porkers at 11sh Each	01	02	00
Jan 12	Sold him a Red Cow & 2 Piggs out of the Yard	05	05	00
1737				
Apr 18	2 Lambs at 9sh Each	00	18	00
May	2 Calves at 1 10 0 Each	03	0	00
Jul	1 Lamb at 10 sh	00	10	00
Aug 1	a side of Lamb	00	05	00
Aug 6	another Lamb at 10 sh	00	10	00
Aug 11	a side of Mutton at 5 sh	00	05	00
Aug 15	another Lamb from Sheephall	00	10	00
Aug 25	2 Porkers at 2 sh per stone at	02	04	00

[73] Mr Betham came to supply the Cure at Datchworth at Midsummer 1714

Dec 21	Paid Mr Betham myselfe	01	10	00
24	Paid him by Order on William Blindall	05	00	00
	Paid him by Order on Robert Flindall	02	10	00
[1714/15]				
Feb 27	Paid him by Order on Michael Ireland	02	10	00
1715				
Jul 12	Paid him more myselfe	01	00	00
Aug 12	Paid him more myselfe	10	00	00
Sep 18	Paid him by Order on Daniel Crawley	02	10	00
	[blank] by Order on John Whitfield	02	10	00
[1715/16]				
Jan 10	Paid him myselfe at Clay hill	05	00	00
	Mr Betham had a Load of Pease	00	12	00
1716				
Jun 16	Paid him at several times six pounds	06	00	00
Aug 17	Paid him more myselfe	01	01	06
Nov 20	Paid him at several times five pounds	05	00	00

1716/17

Feb 15	Paid him more eleven pounds	11	00	00

1717

Aug 12	Paid him myselfe	02	03	00
Oct 26	Paid him by Order on Rowland Mardell & selfe	05	00	00

[1717/18]

Feb 15	Paid him by Order on Mr Miles & selfe	11	00	00
Feb 19	Paid him myselfe	02	01	00

1718

Apr 14	Paid him myselfe ten pounds	10	00	00
	Total of the above particulars	86	07	06

[74] *Notes about tithes, hedges, wood, sheep etc.*

1715/16 Tythes due from Thomas Hills	00	*[blank]*	
from Widowe Mardell	00	15	00
From John Mardell	00	03	00
From Thomas Mansell	00	04	00
from John Ginn	00	02	00
From Daniel Ginn 6 years	00	02	00
From Edward Pennyfather	00	07	00
From Thomas Kimpton senr	00	*[blank]*	
From Benjamine Uncle	00	*[blank]*	

Hedging at Datchworth 1716

For the new Quick set[111] in the further Field Flindall & Tyler 750 setts at 6d [*per 100*]	00	03	09
for planting them etc [*Written beside the amount:* pd]	00	06	00
for 2 men one Day mending hedges	00	02	00
42 Pole of Hedging round the Orch[ar]d	01	01	00
25 Pole of Hedging in the Lower Field by Mrs Kimpton's Field by Tyler	00	12	06

---

[111] quickset: a young plant usually hawthorn used for hedges

330 Faggotts at 20d per 100	[*5s 6d*]	00 05 05
3 Days work on Hedging		00 03 00
For Thorns of Wallis		00 10 00
Naysh & Ray for fetching them		00 04 00
2 Days Work my Horses		00 06 00
Tyler one Days Work in the Church Yard		00 01 00
Tyler made in the Berry Woods		[*blank*]
Tyler made in the Wood		[*blank*]
I bought of Mr King Faggott 510		
Sep 30 1711 pd John Flindall for Bushes		00 04 00

April 20 1719

Memorandum Goodman Titmus then told me that there was 40 Pole of Wood fell'd in the Berry Woods last Season so that there is four Pole due to me which they will pay me next Year   William Hawtayne

Joseph Roberts & Titmus fell'd thes 40 Poles

Thomas Goose shore June 10 1719 an 100 sheep 49 more that were not shorn of one Wall[i]s a sheep chafferer 39 of his own lately bought in. Wallis shore 36 sheep, [I] had 3 fleeces[112]

Sowed 4 Bushill of Saint Foine[113] upon an Acre with 3 or 4 pounds of Clover seed

Feb 1 1716/17

Edward Mardell has two Years Quitt Rent[114] in his hands demands 3 Years to the next Lady Day. Quitt Rent is 2 shillings a Years

---

[112] chafferer: a trader

[113] saint foine: saintfoin, or sainfoin: a low growing perennial herb, also lucerne

[114] quit rent: rent (usually small) paid by a freeholder or copyholder in lieu of services which might otherwise be required

TITHE ACCOUNTS

[1] *First legible page in the account book concerning haymaking. It is preceded by a badly torn page containing some illegible entries.*

Saturday 23 June 1711

Goodman Harwood six Days		0 07 0
His Wife 5 Days		0 03 4
His Youngest Daughter 5 Days		0 03 4
~~His Eldest Daughter~~	[*Total*]	00 13 8
Brought from the other side[115] for making		00 03 4
Hay at Mr Bouchier's Farm		01 05 0
and Mr Nicholls's Field		01 05 6
For hay making there the Totall		03 07 6
Paid Goodman Waple for mowing 17 Acres		01 14 0
Paid his Wife for haymaking since in the parsonage Field at Ellstree		00 01 6
	[*Total*]	05 03 0

---

[115] Probably refers to the previous torn page

APPENDIX

Appendix 1: Datchworth Glebe Terrier 1607[116]

Datchworth alias Thatchworth rectoria, March 27[th] ano dom 1607.
A survey or terrier of all the possessions belonging to the rectorie of Datchworth alias Thatchworth in the Countie of Hertford and Diocese of Lincoln made and taken by the view p[er]ambulation and estimate of the minister, Churchwardens Sidesmen and other the inhabitants there whose names are subscribed, being therunto nominated and appoynted by William Folkingham gent' generall surveyeur of Church gleabes & possessions within the diocese of Lincolne by vertue of a Commission decreed by the Reverend Father in God William, Lord Bishopp of Lincoln in execution of the Canon in that behalfe established.

In Primis there is belonging unto the said rectorie one dwellinge house covered with tyles, scituate uppon partes of the glebelands belonging to the sayde rectorie. The cheifest parte of the building whearof is 62 foote longe north and south and 18 foote broade East and West. Wich is devided into 2 storyes, conteyninge 10 roomes whearof 5 ar uppon the grounde viz: one little lodginge chamber, one seller, one hall, one parlor, and one butterye and 5 roomes over these viz: one chamber over the seller and little lowe chamber, one chamber over the hall with a closett or studye belonginge to it & one chamber over the parlor with a closett or studye over it wich is over the butterye.

Item one othe part or parcell of the sayde dwelling house adjoyneth with the forenamed parte & is 35 foote longe East and West and 14 foote broade which containeth 4 roomes viz: one kitchin & a brew-house on the grounde & 2 chambers boorded over the kitchin.

Item there is neere adjoyninge unto the foresayde dwelling house one other parcell of buildinge covered with straw or thatch and is in length 44 foote East & West & 15 foote broade devided into 3 severall roomes uppon the grounde & one roome at the west end hath a chamber boorded over it.

Item not far from the foresayde parcell of buildinge there is an other parcell of buildinge covered also with strawe or thatch & is 19 foote long East & West and 16 foote broade wich is devided into 2 roomes uppon the grounde & that roome which is on the west end of this building hath a chamber boorded over it.

---

[116]HALS: DP/33/1/1

APPENDIX

Item there is one large barn covered with straw or thatch which is 94 foote long north & south & 24 foote broade and is divided into 5 bayes.[117]

Item there is one other little barne covered with thatch or straw which is 34 foote longe East & West & 15 foote broad & is divided into 2 bayes.

Item there is lyinge about the forsayde buildings belonginge to the forsayd Rectorie 10 acres of Lande more or lesse, wich is devided into several parcells viz: one garden, one Orcharde, one yarde called the barne-yarde lying between the great barn and the Mansion House & other yards for wood etc: also 2 closes of arable lande & one cloase of pasture called the Springe. All wich beinge conjoyned together, abutt upon a lane leadinge from Thatchworth Greene towards Knebworth on the North, On the land of Sir Rowland Litton Knight belonging to Mardly Bury in the South. On the lands of Richard Rudd East and a lane leading from Thatchworth Church toward Wolmer greene west.

Item there belonge unto the sayd rectorie 6 acres of arable land more or lesse, lying in a common feild there called Cundell[118] whearof one acre and a halfe more or less lyeth betweene the lands of George Shotboult[119] South & the lands of Thomas Kimpton North & abutteth upon the lane wich leadeth from Brackburie ende[120] to Thatchworth Church East, & the lands of Richard Kimpton West.
And one other part in the sayd feild, contayning one acre more or less lyeth betweene the lands of Thomas Kimpton South and the lands of Thomas Foster North: and abutteth upon the forsayde lane leading from Brackburie End to Thatchworth Church East, & the lands of Thomas Foster West.
And one other part in the forsayd common feild contayning one acre & halfe more or less lyeth between the forenamed lane which leadeth from Brackburie End to Thatchworth Church East & the lands of Richard Rudd on the West & abutteth uppon sayd lane north & uppon the land of Francis Bigg South.
And one other part in the forsayd common feild contayning by estimation one acre more or less lyeth between the lands of Thomas Foster West and the lands

---

[117] This may have been a tithe barn, however, no supporting evidence has been found
[118] HALS: DE/AS/1435, Indenture dated 20 April 1843 refers to 'a Common Field fomerly called Cundell and now Slidingdale'
[119] 'Shotbolt' occurs once in the tithing book **[69]**. The name 'Shadbolt' may be found today
[120] Bragbury End

of William Rudd East, & abutteth uppon the land of John Man North & of Francis Bigg South.

And one other piece in the forsayd common feild contayning one acre more or less lyeth between the land of John Man East & West & abutteth uppon a parcell of medow of the sayd John Mans & others etc North & uppon the lands of Thomas Kimpton South.

And one other parcell of lande in the forsayd common feild contayning halfe an acre more or less lyeth between the lands of John Man north & of John Deards South & abutteth uppon the land of the forsayd John Man etc East & West.

Item there belongs unto the sayd rectorie 4 acres of arable land lying in a common feild of the forsayd parish called Chibdens: whearof 3 acres more or less lye between the lands of Thomas Mitchell on the south, & the lands of the sayd Thomas Mitchell & Thomas Kimpton north & abutt upon the lands of the sayd Thomas Mitchell west, & of the sayd Thomas Kimpton East.

And one other parte in the foresayde common feilde contayning halfe an acre more or lesse lyeth betweene the lands of George Kimpton East, & the lands of Charles North West, & abutteth uppon the lands of the sayde George Kimpton South & of Richard Kimpton North.

And one other part in the forsayd common feild contayning halfe an acre more or less lyeth between the lands of Richard Kimpton on the South & the land of Thomas Mitchell & Thomas Foster North: & abutteth uppon the lands of the sayd Thomas Mitchell west & the land of Richard Kimpton East.

[signed]William Paine parson of Thatchworth[121]

      Charles North (gent)
      William North
      Thomas Foster   Thomas Waterman ⎫
      Edward Mitchell   Thomas Mitchell   ⎬ Churchwardens
                                      ⎭

---

[121] William Payne was rector of Datchworth from 1600-22 (Beachcroft, *Five Hide Village*, p58). A memorial brass plate to him is in Datchworth church near the altar rail

APPENDIX

Appendix 2: Noteworthy landowners and tenants

[*Unless stated otherwise, references to burials are from Datchworth Parish registers HALS: DP/33/1/1 or DP/33/1/2*].

William Butterfield paid tithes regularly throughout the period. In the early years he rented Hawkins Hall from a Mrs Knight, whose connection with Edmund Knight who bought the hall in 1673 is not known.[122] Associated with the hall were 50 acres of land. Butterfield's tithes gradually increased until they reached a peak of £8 10s in 1727 **[44]**. However, by 1742 he was paying just 1s for 'Dell Close' **[60]**. In 1746, Thomas Neots 'of Hawkins Hall' **[65]** was paying £4 for tithes, a payment that had started in 1742, the same year that William Butterfield probably left Hawkins Hall.

Daniel Crawley paid tithes consistently from 1713 to 1728. The entry in the tithe book in 1724 suggests that by then he had connections with Bragbury End Farm **[42]**. Although land tax records show that he rented land from several landlords in different parts of Datchworth, their whereabouts is not revealed. He was overseer of the poor in 1713 and 1727. He married Elizabeth Wallis of Bramfield in 1704 and their son John was born in 1710.[123]
When Daniel died aged 60 in 1729 he was described as 'yeoman'.[124] His widow, Elizabeth, continued to pay small tithes, turnips and rent for 'a piece of glebe in Rush Mead' until 1734 **[51, 52, 53]**. Her son John continued and from 1741 until 1747 paid a composition tithe of £16 per year. There were, apparently, two John Crawleys in Datchworth. One rented property in Burnham Green **[12]**, and was labelled as such presumably to distinguish him from the John Crawley who was son of Daniel and Elizabeth Crawley.

William Dardes/Deards lived at Deards End in Knebworth Parish, and farmed about 45 acres of land in Datchworth. The entry in 1721 'by his Bill for meat' **[39]**, hinted that he was a butcher, confirmed by his will in 1736[125]. John Deards, who may have been William's son, did not pay tithes in Datchworth but, like William, was a butcher judging by his dealings with Hawtayne **[72]** from 1735 to 1737. A variety of animals was sold to Deards, and occasionally

[122] Beachcroft, *Five Hide Village*, p68
[123] IGI
[124] B Crawley, S Flood and C Webb, *Wills at Hertford 1415-1858* (British Record Society Limited, 2007), p136
[125] Crawley, *Wills at Hertford*, p151

sides of meat were purchased by Hawtayne. It gives another dimension to Hawtayne's farming activities. The family name of Dardes dates from the fourteenth century and its variation of Deards is the origin of Deards End, an area in Knebworth.[126] It is no surprise, then, that the name appears in the Datchworth Glebe Terrier of 1607 (see Appendix 1).

John Flindall leased Swangleys Farm from 1701 for 21 years, but died in 1713 before the lease expired.[127] His son, Robert, agreed a composition of £9 10s in 1715 **[26]**. Other members of the family paid tithes from time to time, Samuel **[35]**, who was Robert's brother **[14]**, also Joshua and Robin. The family left the farm when the lease expired. Another John Flindall lived in Datchworth, as noted by Hawtayne **[9]**.

William Game appeared in the village in 1728 according to land tax and tithe records. He was assessed for tax on two counts, one in his own right and the other for 'Mardall's land' which he rented. The former amount was probably for Raffin Green Farm as at this date, the owner, Robert King, was relieved of paying the land tax for Raffin Green. Land tax records also indicate that Game acquired more land in 1732. His annual tithe payments increased from £4 10s initially to £9 in 1740. There is further confirmation of his connection with Raffin Green Farm in the entries for 1744 **[62]** and 1745 **[64]** where he is described as being 'of Raffing Green Farm'. He served as church warden for seven consecutive years from 1736. In his will, dated 1754, he was described as a farmer.[128]

Edward Harrison of Balls Park, Hertford, bought Datchworthbury in 1719 and owned it until his death in 1732, when it passed to his daughter, Audrey.[129] Datchworthbury stayed in the hands of the Townshend family at least until 1791.[130] Harrison does not appear in the tithing book but the assessment for paying poor relief in 1721 reveals the names of some of his tenants (Appendix 5).

---

[126] WEA, *Knebworth,* p12
[127] WEA, *Knebworth*, p13
[128] Crawley, *Wills at Hertford*, p211
[129] She was the wife of Charles Townshend, the son of Viscount Townshend, (known as 'Turnip Townshend') who lived at Balls
[130] Page, *VCH Hertfordshire,* Volume III, p79

APPENDIX

Thomas Kimpton took over the tenancy of Swangleys Farm in 1725 on a 21 year lease.[131] Swangleys Farm was part of the Lytton estate in Knebworth, tenants of which farmed land in Datchworth throughout Hawtayne's incumbency. Kimpton paid a composition of £12 6s up to 1731 and from 1732 he was paying £21 per year. He reverted to small tithe payments in 1737 and 1738 when the price of wheat was low, then, apart from one or two lapses, he paid c£20 until 1745, when the lease expired. Kimptons were tenants in the open fields over 100 years earlier as described in the Datchworth Glebe Terrier of 1607 (Appendix 1).

William Kimpton was one of Robert King's tenants in the early years of Hawtayne's incumbency. He is first mentioned as holding land 'of Robert King Esq at Raffin Green' **[14]** and an entry concerning Kimpton's tithes 'of Mr King's Farm at Raffin Green' **[18]** suggests that Kimpton's tenancy included the farm as well as the land. This land amounted to 44 acres and more than half of it was south of the farm along the parish border. Two fields called Little and Upper Swangleys shared their name with Swangleys Farm on the western side of the parish in the detached part of Knebworth. It is possible that these fields once belonged to the farm, but no evidence for this has been found. Until 1724 Kimpton paid a fairly consistent annual tithe of £4 10s, the same amount as paid by his predecessor Thomas Coulson **[18]**, but his land tax payments were concluded in 1723. So his tenancy ceased sometime during 1723 to 1724. No record of his burial or will has been found.

Robert King was paying land tax in two parts in 1715, on his own behalf and for his tenant at Raffin Green Farm **[14]**, William Kimpton. The latter subsequently paid the tax in his own right until 1723 when he ceased to hold the tenancy and King resumed payments. The next tenant was William Game to whom the burden of land tax was then bestowed. Robert King's tithe payments were varied, irregular and usually of modest amounts. The most he paid was £7 5s. The entry for this was 'M̶r̶ Robert King Esq **[43]** as though Hawtayne was not altogether clear about his social status. A mention of 'latter marth hay' from 'Bragher End' **[28]** in 1715 is the first hint that King had associations with Bragbury End in the north of the parish. It was on King's land that nectarines, peaches and hops were being grown in 1715 **[28]**. A puzzling entry refers to John Crawley paying tithe of 2s 'for the Rent of a piece of Glebe Land in Mr King's Rush Mead'. This was probably the northernmost piece of glebe land situated adjacent to a field called 'Little Rush Mead' (see Figure 4). Robert

---

[131] HALS: DE/K/46613

APPENDIX

King 'Esquire' was buried in July 1738, aged 71, in Datchworth church yard where a badly eroded gravestone still remains.[132] Land tax continued to be paid by a Mr King of 'Bragherend' until 1747; his relationship to Robert is uncertain.

William Robinson Lytton was originally William Robinson. Robinson was a distant relative of the Lyttons of Knebworth and after inheriting the estate in c1710, adopted the name Lytton.[133] Datchworth parish contained lands from this estate and a few references are made to 'Esquire'[13] or 'Mr' [14] Lytton in this context. He also paid land tax and was assessed for poor relief contributions (see Appendices 3 and 4). On his death in 1732, he was succeeded by his son, John Robinson Lytton [67]. Rowland Lytton, mentioned in the Datchworth Glebe Terrier of 1607 (see Appendix 1), succeeded to the family estate in 1582 and died in 1615. Successions in the male line continued until 1705 when the estate passed to a great nephew and eventually to William Robinson.[134]

William Lytton [37] and **[38]** was rector at Knebworth from 1704 until 1730. His relationship with the Lytton family is unknown.[135]

Rowland Mardell owned Bridgefoot Farm from about 1715. The farm consisted of 41½ acres **[13]**. The previous owner had been John Randall who had agreed to a composition of £5 in 1712 **[9]** but died soon after.[136] Rowland Mardell paid up to £1 for 'small tithes and turnips' until 1730. He had the distinction of paying nothing for several years and then paying eight retrospective payments of £1 in 1725. He had property at West End, near the border of Knebworth parish; his tenant was Thomas Freeman who appears in the tithe accounts until 1717. He was overseer of the poor in 1716 and constable in 1731. He died in 1747.

William Wallis owned Datchworthbury at the time of Hawtayne's induction in 1709, having bought it in 1693. Over the next few years he continued his property investment by buying the manor house of Wormleybury and houses in

---

[132] A Ruston, (ed), *Hertfordshire monumental inscriptions, Datchworth, the parish church of All Saints*, (Hertfordshire Family History Society, 2003), p4
[133] Richardson, *Knebworth*, p26
[134] Richardson, *Knebworth*, pp25-26
[135] WEA, *Knebworth*, p10
[136] Crawley, *Wills at Hertford*, p448 and HALS: DE/AS/1886

APPENDIX

the borough of Steyning (Sussex).[137] Wallis was MP for Steyning for four separate periods from 1705 to 1722. By 1719, when he sold Datchworthbury, he was already in financial difficulties and eventually went bankrupt. It seems that he had 'acted as security for the receiver-general of excise ... at the beginning of the reign of Queen Anne and his estate had been seized by the excise authorities'. He died in 1737, aged 80, 'within the rules of the Fleet Prison', meaning that he was technically an inmate but lived in lodgings close to the Prison providing he paid a fee to the keeper.[138] A second William Wallis pays 'small tithes' and 'tithe of turnips' from 1719 to the end of Hawtayne's incumbency in 1747. His connection, if any, with William Wallis MP is not known.

James Whitehall was one of Edward Harrison's tenants at Datchworthbury and paid small tithes from 1722 to 1725. He then became a significant contributor to Hawtayne's funds by paying a fixed sum of £20 per year almost consistently from 1727 to 1736 followed by payments of £2 'for the Berry, small tithes' **[43]** in 1737 and 1738 during a period when the price of wheat was low. Whitehall's £20 payment was restored in 1740 and continued thus until he died aged 76 in 1743.

---

[137] E Cruikshanks, S Handley, D W Hayton, (eds), *The House of Commons* (Cambridge, 2002), Vol V *Members O-Z*, pp767-768
[138] J Gardiner, N Wenborn, (eds), *The History Today Companion to British History,* (1995), p403

APPENDIX

Appendix 3: Burials and wills of Datchworth tithe payers found between 1711 and 1747

Dates of burials and/or wills tabulated below are for Datchworth tithe payers who were buried in Datchworth or one of the surrounding parishes: Aston (Ast), Knebworth (Kne), Walkern (Wal) and Welwyn (Wel). Burials are in Datchworth unless otherwise labelled. Other abbreviations used in will records are: Bragbury End (Brag), Woolmer Green (Wool) and Datchworth (Dat). Forename abbreviations are similar to those that preface the Names Index.

The presentation of parish registers varies in quality according to the parson's handwriting and the arrangement of information therein. Happily, in most of the cases above, burials for each year are grouped together and usually fairly legible, however, a few pages have deteriorated or been damaged. For these reasons, no claim is made that this list is complete and omission does not imply that no record was made.

Surname	Forename	Burial [139]	Will [140]
Adams	Thos	30 July 1743, yeoman (Wel)	1743, yeoman, Welch's (Wel)
Adams	Thos		1745/6 Welch's (Wel)
Adams	Thos	27 Dec 1728, Mr, the younger (Wal)	1729, jun, gent (Wal)
Adams	Thos	13 Jan 1739/40 (Wal)	1740, gent (Wal)
Bassett	John	14 May 1717	1717, John, elder, carpenter (Dat)
Bigg	Fra	8 Aug 1717, aged 58	
Bigg	Wm	2 Sep 1741, aged 94	
Blindall	Jn	3 Aug 1725 (Wel)	1725, yeoman (Wel)
Blindall	Wm	3 Feb 1734/5, aged 85	1734/5, elder, yeoman (Dat)
Cater	Wm	12 Dec 1726 (Ast)	1726/7, yeoman (Ast)
Crawley	Dan	25 Jan 1729/30, aged 60	1729/30, yeoman (Brag)
Crawley	Eliz	15 Apr 1742, aged 70	
Crawley	Eliz	4 Dec 1743, aged 67	
Crawley	Peter		1754, farmer (Dat)

---

[139] HALS: DP/9/1/1; DP/33/1/2; DP/62/1/3; DP/114/1/2; DP/119/1/2
[140] Crawley, *Wills at Hertford*

Deards	Wm	19 sep 1736 (Kne)	1736, butcher, Deards End (Kne)
Draper	Chris	17 Feb 1738/9 (Wel)	
Emmins	Wm	28 May 1737 (Kne)	
Field	Jn	4 Apr 1741, aged 80	1741, husbandman (Dat)
Flindall	Joanna	21 Feb 1716/17, wid (Kne)	
Flindall	Jn	20 Nov 1713 (Kne)	1713, yeoman (Kne)
Flindall	Jn	24 Feb 1716/17 (Kne)	
Flindall	Joshua	13 Jun 1715 (Kne)	
French	Thos	16 Mar 1734/5, aged 40	
Game	Mr		1754, farmer (Dat)
Ginn	Dan	14 Apr 1718, aged 70	
Ginn	Jn	16 Jun 1723, aged 73	
Goose	Jn	8 Oct 1742, aged 66	1742, yeoman (Dat)
Goose	Thos		1754, yeoman (Dat)
Goose	Thos	2 Dec 1721, aged 76	1721, yeoman (Brag)
Grey	Edw	31 Mar 1723, aged 52	
Hatton	Wm	10 Jun 1726, aged 80	
Hewson	Ric	11 Jan 1732/3, aged 60	
Hudson	Jos	15 Jul 1738, aged 73	1738, labourer, (Dat)
Ireland	Mic	8 Jul 1719, aged 90	
Jeaques	Thos	23 Jan 1733/4, aged 80	
Jones	Chas	11 Dec 1723, aged 63, gent	
Kimpton	Alice	24 Mar 1724/5, aged 70	1725, wid (Dat)
Kimpton	Rebecca	11 Jun 1726, wid (Wel)	1726, wid, Mardleybury (Wel)
Kimpton	Thos		1718, yeoman (Dat)
King	Rob	24 July 1738, aged 71, esq	
Langley	Geo	18 Nov 1744, aged 37	
Lytton	Wm Robinson	25 Nov 1732, esq (Kne)	
Lytton	Wm	19 Apr 1736, rector, (Kne)	1737, rector (Kne)
Mansell	Jos	4 Apr 1731, aged 81	
Mardell	Dan	(no date)1747	1747, yeoman (Dat)
Mardell	Edw	21 Aug 1744 (of the parish of Welwyn) (Kne)	1744, senior, farmer (Wool)
Mardell	Jn	3 Aug 1721, aged 32	

APPENDIX

Mardel	Rob	7 Jun 1717, 'kill'd by shoeing a horse'	
Mardel	Rowland	(no date) 1747	
Mardell	Wid	4 Apr 1718, Elizabeth, widow	
Mardell	Wid		1752, Sarah, wid (Wool)
Nash	Thos	7 Mar 1741/2, aged 75, parish clerk	
North	Rob		1713, husbandman (Dat)
Pearce	Jn	27 Aug 1738, aged 41	
Pearce	Jn	18 Jan 1746/7, aged 78	1747, farmer (Dat)
Pendred	Wm	30 Jun 1719, aged 44	
Pennyfather	Wm		1731, gent, Harmer Green (Wel)
Phipp	Jn	19 Aug 1739, aged 67	
Randall	Jn		1712, yeoman (Dat)
Roberts	Jos	11 Jul 1731, aged 57	
Smith	Hen	23 Sep 1728, husbandman (Ast)	
Smith	Jn	16 Mar 1740/1, aged 70	
Uncles	Ste	Jan 1711/12, (Wel)	
Venables	Thos	9 Nov 1739, aged 96	
Webster	Jos		1743, yeomen (Wel)
Whitehall	Jas	18 Sep 1743, aged 76	1744, yeoman (Dat)
Whittenborough	Wm		1741, yeoman (Dat)
Winch	Rob	11 Aug 1719, aged 77	

APPENDIX

Appendix 4: Datchworth Land Tax return for 1721[141]

The original document shows extra columns with quarterly payments. These have been omitted. A column has been added estimating the rent based on the tax rate for 1721 which was 3 shillings in the pound.

Datchworth in the County of Hartford An Assessment made 26 May 1721 for granting An Aide to his magesty King George the Som of [£]121-19-0 shilings Charge upon this parish for the searvices of this yeare 1721

| [Name] | [Notes] | yearly | | | [Rent |
		[£]	[s]	[d]	in £]
Esqr Lytton	for woods	0	9	0	3
Saml Flindall		3	3	0	21
Saml Flindall	Hee for one [own]	0	3	0	1
William Dards		1	10	0	10
Edward Mardall		0	3	0	1
William Emines		3	12	0	24
Mr Hawtanye		13	10	0	90
Mr Milles		15	18	0	106
Joseph Hudson		1	16	0	12
William Bedall		0	18	0	6
Mr Thomas Adams		8	11	0	57
William Blindall		1	16	0	12
William Blindall	hee for Woolmergreen	0	15	0	5
Widow Kimpton		1	13	0	11
Mr Robard King		6	9	0	43
Henery Smeith		3	18	0	26
Thomas Goose		5	14	0	38
Thomas Goose	hee for Whittenbury	2	8	0	16
Thomas Goose	hee for Braches[142]	1	4	0	8
William Kimpton		2	14	0	18
William Wallis		6	3	0	41
John Godfrey		1	10	0	10
Rowland Mardall		3	15	0	25
Mr Knight		3	18	0	26
John Feild		3	18	0	26
Widow Mardall		0	6	0	2

---

[141] HALS: Land Tax, Datchworth
[142] Breeches: field 67 in the Datchworth 1839 tithe award (HALS: DSA4/34/2)

Mr Adleys		2	5	0	*15*
Mr Jones		0	15	0	*5*
Mr William Penyfather		1	10	0	*10*
Mr William Penyfather	hee for Doctor Shotteradges	1	10	0	*10*
John Hawkins		0	12	0	*4*
Danill Crawly		1	10	0	*10*
Danill Crawly	hee for Young Land	0	15	0	*5*
Danill Crawly	hee for Tatnumes Land	1	1	0	*7*
Danill Crawly	hee for feid Craft[143]	0	15	0	*5*
John Titmust		0	12	0	*4*
Thomas Adams		1	4	0	*8*
Francis Kimpton		0	12	0	*4*
John Farr		0	12	0	*4*
Thomas Flint		0	18	0	*6*
William Whittenbury		3	0	0	*20*
Thomas Hilles		0	12	0	*4*
John Mardall		0	6	0	*2*
Thomas Blindall		0	12	0	*4*
Joseph Baldock		0	12	0	*4*
John Gurnney		0	3	0	*1*
William Hadan		0	18	0	*6*
Edward Gray		0	6	0	*2*
Robard Heath		0	9	0	*3*
John Smieth		0	18	0	*6*
Richard Hucsson		0	6	0	*2*
John Phipp		0	12	0	*4*
John Bassett		0	6	0	*2*
John Millard		0	6	0	*2*
Danil Mardall		0	3	0	*1*
Joseph Webster		0	9	0	*3*
Frances Titmust		0	3	0	*1*
John Ginn		0	6	0	*2*
Jeames Blindall		0	3	0	*1*
Thomas Harard		0	9	0	*3*
Thomas Venables		0	9	0	*3*
John Venables		0	9	0	*3*
	[*Correct total is £122 2s 0d*]	121	19	0	

[*Signed*] Daniel Crawley, John Field, John Godfery

---

[143] Field Croft: field 145 in the 1839 Datchworth tithe award

APPENDIX

Appendix 5: Datchworth Poor Relief payments 1721[144]

Vestry Note Book Poor Rate for 1721 at 6d in the £

[Name]	[Notes]	[Yearly]			[Rent in £]
		[£]	[s]	[d]	
Willm Harrison Esq	For his Woods				
Willm Miles	His Tennant for the Berry Farme[145]	2	10	6	101
Willm Wallis	His Tenant	1	0	0	40
John Godfrey	His Tenant	0	5	0	10
Robert King Esq	For Woods	0	1	0	2
Robert King Esq	For his house and meadows	0	10	0	20
Henry Smith	His Tennant	1	3	0	46
Wm Kimpton	His Tennant	0	9	6	19
Wm Robinson	For Woods				
Lytton Esq		0	1	6	3
Wm Dardes	His Tennant	0	4	0	8
Wm Emmins	His Tennant	0	12	0	24
Edd Mardell	Of Woolmore Green His Tennant	0	0	6	1
Saml Flindall	His Tennant for Swangleys Farme	0	15	0	30
Saml Flindall	He for his own Land	0	0	6	1
Saml Flindall	He for the Barnes Closes	0	5	0	10
Wm Blindall	for his owne Wood Land	0	1	0	2
Wm Blindall	He for Land at West End	0	4	0	8
Wm Blindall	He for Coltsfoot Farme	1	6	6	53
Thos Adams	Of Walkerne for his Woods	0	3	0	6
Thos Flint	His Tennant	0	3	6	7
Thos Adams	Of Welches	0	4	0	8
Willm Hawtayne	Rector for Glebe & Tythes	2	5	0	90
Thos Goose	For his own Farme	0	18	0	36
Thos Goose	He for Whittenborough's Land	0	3	6	7
Thos Goose	He for the Braches	0	4	0	8
Rowland Mardell	For the Bridgefoot Land [and] His Tennant at West End	0	12	0	24
Rebeca Kimpton	Widowe	0	5	6	11
Joseph Hudson		0	6	0	12
Willm Butterfield		0	11	6	23
John Field		0	13	0	26

---

[144] HALS: DP/33/8/1
[145] Datchworthbury

Willm Pennyfather	For the Bulls his own[146]	0	5	0	*10*
Willm Pennyfather	He for Dr Shortridges's Land	0	5	0	*10*
Nathaniel Asser		0	7	0	*14*
John Hawkins		0	2	0	*4*
Danl Crawley	For Nashes Land	0	5	0	*10*
Danl Crawley	He for Youngs Land	0	1	6	*3*
Danl Crawley	He for Tatnums Land	0	3	6	*7*
Danl Crawley	He for his own Land	0	2	0	*4*
Alice Kimpton	For her own	0	2	0	*4*
Alice Kimpton	She for Gables Land	0	2	0	*4*
Willm Bedell		0	2	6	*5*
Willm Whittenborough	For Lucas's Land	0	9	0	*18*
Willm Whittenborough	He for Jon Whittenborough's Land	0	2	0	*4*
Thos Venables	junr	0	1	0	*2*
John Venables		0	1	6	*3*
Henry Tingeo		0	1	0	*2*
Robert Heath		0	1	0	*2*
John Ginn		0	1	0	*2*
John Bassett		0	1	0	*2*
Edward Grey		0	1	0	*2*
Thos Harwood		0	1	6	*3*
John Miller		0	0	9	*£1 10s*
John Crawley		0	2	0	*4*
John Phipp		0	2	0	*4*
Joseph Mansell		0	1	0	*2*
John Blindall	Of Woolmore Green	0	0	6	*1*
John Titmasse		0	2	0	*4*
John Smith	At the White House	0	2	6	*5*
John Mardell		0	1	0	*2*
Joseph Baldock		0	1	0	*2*
Thos Hilles	And Landlord for Wood	0	2	0	*4*
Mr Jones		0	2	6	*5*
Willm Skegg		0	1	0	*2*

---

[146] Several fields were called 'Bulls'. The largest was Great Bulls, field 440 in the 1839 Datchworth tithe award when these fields were still in the hands of a William Pennyfather

Appendix 6: Notes about weather and crops taken from J M Stratton's *Agricultural records*[147]

J M Stratton extended some records originally kept by Thomas H Baker who published them in 1883. Baker, who farmed in south-west Wiltshire, had confined his publication to local sources. Stratton, in 1969, added to Baker's assessment in an attempt to broaden the context, and finally, in 1978, Ralph Whitlock brought the record up to date and included agricultural prices.[148] Although not specifically for Hertfordshire, some of the reports are sufficiently general to be of some interest. (* Price of wheat per quarter)

Year	*s	d	Weather	Crops	Other notes
1709	78	6	Bad year, backward spring, general scarcity; severe frost from Jan 1st for 50 days, April & May cold & wet.	Crops suffered; scarcity of grass.	Price of wheat reflected bad harvest last year. Thames froze
1710	78	0		Another famine year; exportation of corn was prohibited for one year.	Winnowing fans introduced in Scotland
1711	54	0	Spring wet & cold, then very dry weather promoted early ripening. Rainfall low in eastern counties.	Wheat cut July 27th & barley Aug 26th.	
1712	46	4	Very dry spring until middle of May; hot spell until June 20th. Strong winds before harvest.		
1713	51	0	Dry year cold spring, drought followed by dry summer.	Wheat good, barley & oats poor crop.	
1714	50	4	One of the driest years on record. Spring cold & dry, summer & autumn dry and hot.	Yield of wheat quite good, oats & barley poor	

---

[147] J M Stratton, *Agricultural records AD220-1977* (R Whitlock (ed), 2nd edition, 1978), pp67-76

[148] Stratton, *Agricultural records*, p5

1715	43	0	Summer cold & wet	Grain spoiled at harvest time by rain.	Thames frozen for three months
1716	48	0	Year of drought.	Hay crop was poor; turnips grown in south of England, a failure.	Turnips were first grown on a field scale in Aberdeenshire
1717	45	8	Spring drought. Showery summer, thunderstorms end of July.	Good year for crops.	
1718	38	10	Summer hot & dry.	Harvest quite good.	
1719	35	0	Hot, dry summer.	Hay harvest poor.	
1720	37	0	Very wet.		
1721	37	6	Moderately good year. Hot dry spell in July.	Good hay making.	
1722	36	0	Spring & early summer rather wet. Autumn, dry.		
1723	34	8	Very dry year. Summer was hot.		
1724	37	0	Nothing special.		
1725	48	6	Jan to April, exceptionally dry. April onwards, long spell of rain & gales.		
1726	46	0	Floods in south of England in early part of year.		
1727	42	0	Nothing special.		
1728	54	6	Heavy rain & floods early on, dry summer.		
1729	46	10	Thunderstorms & great winds.	Harvest reasonably good	
1730	36	6	Unusually dry year.	Harvest excellent.	Viscount Charles Townshend began his improvement schemes in Norfolk.
1731	32	10	Very dry year.	Very good harvest.	
1732	26	8	Another dry year.		
1733	28	4	Dry year.		
1734	38	10	Drought until June. From June exceptionally wet.		Flourishing trade in export of grain & malt.

1735	43	0	Rather wet year.	Corn laid flat & hay spoiled.	
1736	40	4	Wet year.	Much damage to hay and corn	In February, Thames rose to greatest height for 50 years
1737	38	0	Dry after wet start.		Food riots against the export of grain.
1738	35	6	Dry esp. in Aug. & Sept.		
1739	38	0	Rather wet year.	Great damage to crops in Sept.	
1740	50	8	Very cold spring & early summer. Drought.	Harvest late & poor.	
1741	46	8	Hot, dry summer. Autumn fine & mild.	Harvest abundant	
1742	34	0	Very dry year.	Excellent harvest.	
1743	24	10	Very dry year. Rainfall 69% of normal.	Harvest very good.	
1744	24	10	Wet spell in third quarter of the year.	Rain caused much damage to crops.	
1745	27	6	Wet year.	Wasteful harvest, much corn growing out.	Epidemic of rinderpest[149] among cattle. Pastures converted to arable, caused depression in price of grain.
1746	39	0	Very hot dry summer	Heavy yields, particularly of barley.	
1747	34	10	Long dry summer.	Harvest yielded well.	

---

[149] rinderpest: commonly called cattle-plague; it is not the same as foot-and-mouth disease (Ernle, *English Farming*, p372)

APPENDIX

Appendix 7: Hops

In the list of tithe payers for 1715 **[28]**, there is an entry concerning hops. The assumption has been made that the almost illegible squiggle above the '12' is 'li' short for 'librae' meaning pounds. So, 12 lb of hops were said to have a value of £1 4s 0d, that is 2s per pound. To what extent hops were grown in Datchworth is unknown, but in the 1838 tithe award, there were two adjacent fields, each approximately 5 acres, called Hopground and Hopground Field which suggests, that at one time hops were a common crop. For their use as flavouring for beer, they were grown initially in the mid-sixteenth century in counties bordering the Channel and the North Sea from Hampshire to Norfolk.[150] By 1715, although some hops were grown in Hertfordshire, the county was not a major producer when compared with the other hop growing areas in the region such as Suffolk and Essex, where, in 1689, hops in Debden (Essex), were tithed at the rate of ten shillings per acre of hopground.[151]

It is difficult to find a contemporary record of hop values to put the rate of 2s per pound in context. Account books dated 1767 to 1777 in the Felbridge area on the Surrey/Sussex border record values from 1d per pound to 1s 2d per pound. This variation is not a surprise when one learns that crop yields could vary from two to fifteen cwt per acre depending on the vagaries of the weather, pests and diseases.[152] But even the highest of these values is considerably lower than Hawtayne's valuation in 1715. It so happens that 1715 was a cold and wet year; in the early part the Thames froze for three months and later in the year, crops were spoiled by rain (see Appendix 6). Mr King must have been remarkably lucky to harvest hops under these adverse conditions, he also successfully grew peaches and nectarines **[28]**. The scarcity of hops that year may have inflated their value.

---

[150] Hey, *The Oxford Companion*, pp221, 222
[151] H H Lockwood, *Tithe & Other Records of Essex & Barking*, (Essex Record Office, 2006), p14
[152] www.felbridge.org.uk/index.php?p=2_58, the Felbridge and District History Group accessed 14 Sept 2009

Glossary

advowson	right of a patron or institution to appoint a priest to a living to care for the souls in the local population
aftermath	the new growth after the first hay harvest
agistment	depasturing or grazing
Artium Magister, *A M*	Master of Arts
baily	contraction of 'bailiff': one who would oversee the running of a manor or an agricultural estate
bated	rebated or repaid
blew pease	blue peas, another name for common or garden peas
bushel	measuring device that holds four pecks
chafferer	trader
cock	small conical heap of hay or crops such as barley, oats, peas and beans
composition	form of tithe commutation agreed for a fixed period of time
dame	the mistress of the household
diet	food that was given as part payment for farm labourers' work.
edge (etch)	corruption of 'eddish': the crop that followed the tilth crop. The stubble was broken up and ploughed for spring sowing of, usually, barley and oats and/or peas and beans
feeding	see 'herbage'
garden penny	a small amount paid to cover the tithe of garden produce in lieu of tithe in kind
grasse	see 'herbage'
hemp	produce of the plant *cannabis sativa*; used to make rough cloth, ropes and sacking
herbage	pertains to grazing
hide	an area sufficient to support a family for a year
Hock Monday	the second Monday after Easter Sunday
homestall	ground immediately connected with the house
latter marth, also latermarth	see 'aftermath'
lock	probably refers to a chain and metal clasp that could be attached to a halter.

GLOSSARY

miscellany, also miscellane, miscling	a mixture of wheat and rye that provided flour for bread called 'maslin'
modus	Shortened form of *modus decimandi*, a customery fixed payment in lieu of tithing in kind
neat	obsolete form of 'net' (in a financial sense)
petty tithe	small tithe
plough or pail	cattle for ploughing or cattle for milking
pluralist	one who holds two or more benefices simultaneously
porket	young pig
privy tithe	small tithe
quere	probably *quaere,* Latin, meaning to look for or to inquire
quickset	young plant, usually hawthorn used for hedges
quit rent	rent (usually small) paid by a freeholder or copyholder in lieu of services which might otherwise be required
rinderpest	commonly called cattle-plague; it is not the same as foot-and-mouth disease
rouncival peas	kind of marrow-fat peas
saint foin	saintfoin, also sainfoin, low growing perennial herb, also lucerne
shock	several sheaves propped against each other, typically, rye or wheat
stone warden	surveyor of highways, responsible for the upkeep of roads
stook	see shock
tare, tares	leguminous plant similar to vetch
tilt (tilth)	crop of wheat and/or rye sown on previously fallowed land
tod	measure of wool, about 28 pounds
vide contra	'see opposite' (often the opposite page)
wether or weather	male sheep usually castrated and in its second season
whitage	relates to the tithes of milk and butter

Bibliography

Primary sources
Bedfordshire and Luton Archives and Record Service
P91/1/2   Leighton Buzzard Parish Register, 1732-1774

Hertfordshire Archives and Local Studies
AHH/3/1   Archdeaconry of Huntingdon, Hitchin Division
ASA/3/1   Archdeaconry of St Albans
DE/K/46613   21 year lease of Swangleys Farm, 10 March 1725/6
DEAS/1435   Conveyance, 20 July 1853
DEAS/1595   Abstract of title, 1602-1818
DE/Bg/4/155   Drawing by J.C. Buckler c 1835-1840
DE/Od/2   Oldfield, H G, *Hertfordshire Topography*, (c 1800), vol 2
DP/8/3/1   Aspenden tithe book, 1722-1753
DP/9/1/1   Aston parish register, 1558-1812
DP/13/3/3   Barkway & Reed tithe book, 1741-1922
DP/14/3/3   Pages from Barley tithe book, 1737-1748
DP/16/3/1   East Barnet & High Barnet tithe book, 1719-1769
DP/30/3/2   Clothall tithe book, 1747-1751
DP/33/1/1   Datchworth parish register, 1570-1724
DP/33/1/2   Datchworth parish register, 1709-1783
DP/33/3/1   Tithe and glebe accounts, 1711-1747
DP/33/8/1   Datchworth vestry book, 1701-1779
DP/33/26/1   Enclosure map and award, Datchworth & Knebworth, 1867
DP/33/29/2   Parish map of Datchworth, 1829
DP/36/1/1   Elstree parish register, 1656-1757
DP/36/3/1   Plan of Rectory Farm, Elstree, 1870, with a note added later referring to the 1776 enclosure
DP/53/1/3   Hitchin parish register, 1679-1746/7, including a 1700 terrier
DP/62/1/3   Knebworth parish register, 1703-1848
DP/78/3/2   Furneux Pelham tithe book, 1729-1764
DP/98/3/3   Sawbridgeworth tithe book, 1686-1723
DP/100/1/1   Shephall parish register, 1560-1735
DP/105/3/2   Memorandum book of Reverend Nicholas Cholwell of Stevenage including a copy of a 1706 glebe terrier

BIBLIOGRAPHY

DP/106/1/2	Tewin parish register, 1718-1812, including a copy of an 1815 terrier
DP/108/3/2	Thorley tithe and glebe account book, 1711-1909
DP/114/1/2	Walkern parish register, 1680-1812
DP/114/3/7	Walkern tithe book, 1740-1749
DP/114/3/9	Walkern tithes, 1735-1783
DP/119/1/2	Welwyn parish register, 1703-1783
DP/120/3/4	Westmill tithe book, 1669-1715
DSA4/34/1-2	Datchworth tithe map and award, 1839
QPE 6-12	Datchworth poll books
Microfilm	Land Tax and Window Tax, Datchworth
Newspapers	Report of Datchworth Rectory fire, *Stevenage Gazette*, 11 Aug 1977 and *Herts Mercury*, 12 Aug 1977

Contemporary books and tracts

Chauncy, Sir Henry, *The Historical Antiquities of Hertfordshire,* (1826), vol 2

Degge, Sir Simon, *The Parson's Counsellor with the Law of Tithes or Tithing* (1676)

Hawtayne, W, *Thanksgiving Sermon on the accession to the throne of George I, 20 January 1715* (Printed for Tim Goodwin, at the Queen's Head against St Dunstan's Church in Fleetstreet, 1715)

Hawtayne, W, *Assizes Sermon at Hertford, 16 July 1716* (Printed for R Burleigh in Amen-Corner, 1716)

Salmon, N, *The History of Hertfordshire Describing the County and its Antient Monuments*, (1728)

Later editions and compilations

Bedfordshire Parish register Series, Volumes 31-33 (BLARS)

Crawley, B, Flood, S & Webb, C, *Wills at Hertford 1415-1858* (British Record Society, 2007)

Defoe, D, *A Tour through England and Wales*, (Everyman's Library, 1928), vol. 2

Doree, S G (ed) *The parish and tithing book of Thomas Hassall of Amwell,* (Hertfordshire Record Society, vol V, 1989)

Leighton Buzzard Terrier (1709), transcript of, (BLARS: CRT 170/2/15/2)

Ruston, A, (ed), *Hertfordshire monumental inscriptions, Datchworth, the parish church of All Saints*, (Hertfordshire Family History Society, 2003)

Savage, A, *The Anglo-Saxon Chronicles,* (2002)

BIBLIOGRAPHY

Secondary sources: books (unless otherwise stated the place of publication is London)

Beachcroft, T O & Emms W B, *Five Hide Village*, (Datchworth Parish Council, 1984)

Bristow, J, *The Local Historian's Glossary & Vade Mecum* (Nottingham, 1994)

Clarke, H W, *A History of Tithes* (1894)

Cockburn, J S, *A history of English assizes 1558-1714*, (Cambridge, 1972)

Coleman S and Wood J, *Historic landscape and archaeology glossary of terms,* (Bedfordshire, 1985)

Cowper, W, *The Poetical Works of William Cowper with a memoir by Charles Whitehead* (1849)

Cruikshanks, E, Handley, S & Hayton, D W, (eds), *The House of Commons* (Cambridge, 2002), vol. V, *Members O-Z*

Cussans, J E, *History of Hertfordshire*, (1870-81, reprinted Yorkshire 1972), vol. III

Ernle, Lord (R E Prothero), *English Farming Past and Present,* (1927)

Evans, E J, *The Contentious Tithe,* (1976)

Foster, J, (ed) *Alumni Oxonienses 1500-1714*, (Oxford, 1891), vol II

Foster, C F, *Four Cheshire townships in the 18th century, Arley, Appleton, Stockton Heath and Great Budworth* (Cheshire, 1992)

Friar, S, *The Local History Companion,* (Stroud, 2001)

Gardiner, J & Wenborn, N, (eds), *The History Today Companion to British History,* (1995)

Hart, A T, *The Country Priest in English History,* (1959)

Hey, D, *The Oxford Companion to Local and Family History*, (Oxford, 1996)

Hindle, P, *Roads and Tracks for Historians*, (Sussex, 2001)

Hollowell, S, *Enclosure Records*, (Chichester, 2000)

Kain, J P & Prince, H C, *Tithe Surveys for Historians,* (2000)

Lockwood, H H, *Tithe & Other Records of Essex & Barking*, (Essex Record Office, 2006)

Lysons, D, *The environs of London, Volume 4, Counties of Herts, Essex & Kent* (1796)

Munby, L M, *Hertfordshire Population Statistics 1563-1801,* (Hertfordshire Local History Council 1964)

Munby, L M, *The common people are not nothing, conflict in religion and politics in Hertfordshire, 1575-1780,* (Hertfordshire, 1995)

Orwin, C S & C S, *The open fields* (Oxford 1967)

Page, W, (ed), *The Victoria County History of the Counties of England, a History of Hertfordshire,* vol III, (1908)

BIBLIOGRAPHY

Page, W, (ed), *The Victoria County History, A History of the County of Bedfordshire,* Vol III, (1912)

Plumb, J H, *The Four Georges*, (1956)

Richardson, J, *The Local Historian's Encyclopedia,* (1986)

Richardson, F A, *Knebworth, the story of a Hertfordshire village*, (Hertford, 1982)

Stratton, J M, *Agricultural records AD220-1977*, (R Whitlock (ed), 2nd edition, 1978)

Tarver, A, *Church court records: an introduction for family and local historians,* (Chichester, 1995)

Tate, W E, *The Parish Chest*, (Cambridge, 1969)

Tiller, K, *English Local History: an Introduction*, (Gloucestershire, 2002)

Urwick, W, *Non conformity in Hertfordshire being lectures upon the nonconforming worthies of St Albans and memorials of Puritanism and Nonconformity in all the parishes of the county of Hertford*, (1884)

Venn, J & J A, *Alumni Cantabrigienses*, (Cambridge, 1922), vol II & (1924) vol III

Venn, J A, *Foundations of Agricultural Economics*, (Cambridge, 1933)

Workers Educational Association, *Knebworth, the story of our village*, (Knebworth, 1967)

Secondary sources: articles

Bowden, P J, 'Statistics', in J Thirsk, (ed), *The Agrarian History of England and Wales*, vol V, 1640-1750, (Cambridge, 1985)

Constable, G, 'Monastic Tithes from their Origin to the Twelfth Century', *Cambridge Studies in Medieval Life and Thought*, new series, X, (1964)

Dixon, S, 'Quakers and the London parish 1670-1720', *The London Journal*, vol 32, no 3, (Nov 2007)

Evans, E J, 'Tithes'in J Thirsk, (ed), *The agrarian history of England and Wales,*vol. V *1640-1750,* (Cambridge 1985)

Evans, E J, 'Tithing Customs and Disputes: the Evidence of Glebe Terriers, 1698-1850', *The Agricultural History Review,* 18.1 (1970)

Heath, C, 'Pride and Justice, Pomp and Pleasure, A Social History' in *The Restoration of Shire Hall Hertford*, (Hertfordshire County Architects, 1990)

Hunt, H G, 'Land tax assessments', in K M Thompson, (ed), *Short guides to records* (The Historical Association, 1994)

Oates, J, Hertfordshire and the Jacobite Rebellions of 1715 and 1745', *Herts Past & Present,* 3rd series, (Spring 2004)

BIBLIOGRAPHY

Pemberton, W A, 'A parson's account book', *The Local Historian,* vol.3, 7 (1979)

Tupling, G H, 'Terriers and Tithe and Enclosure Awards', *The Amateur Historian*, vol I, 12, (c1952-1955)

THE HERTFORDSHIRE RECORD SOCIETY

The Hertfordshire Record Society exists to make Hertfordshire's historical records of all kinds more readily available to the general reader. Since 1985 a regular series of texts has been published.

ALAN THOMSON, Chairman
HEATHER FALVEY, Hon. Secretary
GWYNNETH GRIMWOOD, Hon. Treasurer
SUSAN FLOOD, Hon. General Editor

Membership enquiries and orders for previous publications to the Hon. Treasurer, 50 Sollershott Hall, Sollershott East, Letchworth SG6 3PW

Annual Subscription (2010-2011)   £17.50

Previous publications:

HERTFORDSHIRE RECORD SOCIETY

IX: *St Albans Wills, 1471-1500*. Edited by Susan Flood (1993)   O/P

X: *Early Churchwardens' Accounts of Bishops Stortford, 1431-1538*. Edited by Stephen G Doree (1994)   Price £6.00

XI: *Religion in Hertfordshire, 1847-1851*. Edited by Judith Burg (1995) Price £6.00

XII: *Muster Books for North & East Hertfordshire, 1580-1605*. Edited by Ann J King (1996)   Price £6.00

XIII: *Lifestyle & Culture in Hertford: Wills and Inventories, 1660-1725*. Edited by Beverly Adams (1997)   Price £6.00

XIV: *Hertfordshire Lay Subsidy Rolls, 1307 and 1334*. Edited by Janice Brooker and Susan Flood, with an introduction by Dr Mark Bailey (1998)   Price £6.00

XV: *'Observations of Weather' The Weather Diary of Sir John Wittewronge of Rothamsted, 1684-1689*. Edited by Margaret Harcourt Williams and John Stevenson (1999)   Price £19.00 (£15.00)

XVI: *Survey of the Royal Manor of Hitchin, c1676*. Edited by Bridget Howlett (2000)   Price £18.75 (£15.00)

XVII: *Garden-Making and the Freeman family A Memoir of Hamels, 1713-1733*. Edited by Anne Rowe (2001) Price £18.50 (£15.00)

XVIII: *Two Nineteenth Century Hertfordshire Diaries, 1822-1849*. Edited by Judith Knight and Susan Flood (2002) Price £19.50 (£15.00)

XIX: *"This little commonwealth": Layston parish memorandum book, 1607-c1650 & 1704-c1747*. Edited by Heather Falvey and Steve Hindle (2003)   Price £21.00 (£15.00)

XX: *Julian Grenfell, soldier and poet: letters and diaries, 1910-1915*. Edited by Kate Thompson (2004)   Price £22.00 (£15.00)

XXI: *The Hellard Almshouses and other Stevenage Charities, 1482-2005*. Edited by Margaret Ashby (2005)   Price £21.00 (£15.00)

HERTFORDSHIRE RECORD SOCIETY

XXII: *A Victorian Teenager's Diary: the Diary of Lady Adela Capel of Cassiobury, 1841-1842.* Edited by Marian Strachan (2006)
Price paperback £9.99

XXIII: *The Impact of the First Civil War on Hertfordshire, 1642-1647.* Edited by Alan Thomson (2007)   Price £22.00 (£17.50)

XXIV: *The Diary of Benjamin Woodcock Master of the Barnet Union Workhouse, 1836-1838.* Edited by Gillian Gear (2008)
Price £22.00 (£17.50)

Maps:

The County of Hertford From Actual Survey by A Bryant In the Years 1820 and 1821 (2003)   Price £7.50

A Topographical Map of Hartford-Shire by Andrew Dury and John Andrews, 1766 (2004)   Price £9.50

For more information visit www.hrsociety.org.uk

INDEX OF NAMES

Note: references in Roman numerals refer to pages in the Introduction; references in **bold type** refer to the page numbers of the account book assigned by the editor; references in *italics* refer to page numbers in the Appendices.

Footnotes are signified by fn, preceded by a page number, eg xviiifn or **25fn** (for footnotes relating to a page in the account book)

The following abbreviations have been used:
Ben, Benjamin; Capt, Captain; Cath, Catherine; Chas, Charles; Chris, Christopher; Dan, Daniel; Dat, Datchworth; Edw, Edward; Eliz, Elizabeth; Fra, Francis; Geo, George; gent, gentleman; gdmn, goodman; Hen, Henry; Jas, James; Jn, John; Jos, Joseph; jnr, junior; Kne, Knebworth; Mic, Michael; Nat, Nathaniel; Ric, Richard; Rob, Robert; Sam, Samuel; snr, senior; Thos, Thomas; wid, widow; Wm, William

116

INDEX OF PLACES AND SUBJECTS

Note: references in Roman numerals refer to pages in the Introduction; references in **bold type** refer to the page numbers of the account book assigned by the editor; references in *italics* refer to page numbers in the Appendices.

Footnotes are signified by fn, preceded by a page number, eg xxxfn, or **8fn** (for footnotes relating to a page in the account book)

Unless otherwise stated all towns and villages mentioned are in Hertfordshire.

Produce and animals are listed under the headings 'crops' and 'livestock', however, if William Hawtayne used the word 'tithe' to describe them (eg tithe of turnips or a tithe pig), they are listed under 'tithe'.

INDEX OF PLACES AND SUBJECTS

gaols, xx

garden **61-2**; penny, xxxi

gentleman (description in will), *95-7*

Germany, xvii, xxv

Ginns, **55**

glebe, xxiv-xxv, xxvii, xxxvi-xxxvii,
xxxix, xli-xliv, xlvii, l-lii, lvii, **2, 5,
15, 18, 22, 24, 30, 33-6, 51-7, 63,
65, 67**, *87, 90, 92, 100*; terrier, xv,
xxvii, xxxiii-xxxvi, xxxvii-xxxix,
xliii, *91-3*

Govers Green, ix, **11, 64**

Granborough (Buckinghamshire),
xxxii-xxxiii, xxxix

Greeks, xxii

Green End, **12**; Lane, **13**

Gun, The, **55**

Hampshire, *105*

Harmer Green, **13, 40, 49, 57, 62, 65,**
97

harvest home dinner, **3**

Hawkin's Hall, **12, 65**, *90*

haycock, xxviii

hearth penny, xxxi

hedges:
  bushes, **74**
  quick set, **74**
  thorns, **74**

herbage, xxxiv

Hertford (Hartford), ix, xx-xxi, **4-8, 11,
17-19**; Castle, xx; market, xlvi, **15**;
Sessions House, xx; Shire Hall, xx

Hertfordshire, viii-ix, xiv, xviii, xx,
xxii, xxxvii, xxxix, xliv-xlvi
  Hertford (county of), *87, 98*

hides, ix, xxiv

Hitchin, xx, xxxvii, xxxviii, xxxix

Hock Monday, xxxiii

hog, *see* livestock: pig

honey, xxxiii, xxxviii

Hoppers End Farm, **10, 37**

Idelstrey, Idilstree, *see* Elstree

impropriator(s), xxvi-xxvii

Italy, xviii, xxiii

Jacobite(s), xix, xxi

Jerusalem, xxii

Kent, xx

Kings College (Cambridge), xvii

kitchen, *87*

Knebworth, xliv, **9, 14, 37-8**, *88, 91-3,
96*

Lammas, xxxiii, xxxvi

land tax, li-liii, lv, *90-3,98*

land value, liii-liv

largesse, **3**

Lateran Council (Third, 1179), xxvi
  (Fourth, 1215), xxvi

lattermarth, *see* aftermath and crops:
hay

Laxton (Nottinghamshire), xxxiii

Leighton Buzzard (Bossard) (Beds), xv,
xvi, xxxvi, xxxix, lii, **71**; All Saints
church, xv, xvi

Lilley, **67**

Lincoln, xii; Diocese of, *87*

litigation, xxix

livestock:
  cattle, xxix-xxxii, xliv
    calf (calves), xxvii, xxxi-xxxii,
    xxxiv-xxxvi, xxxviii-xxxix, **72**,
    see also tithe
  cow(s), xxx, xxxiii-xxxiv, xxxvi,
  xxxviii, lvi, **53, 60, 66, 70**
    barren, xxxvi
    fruitful, xxxvi
    grazing, xxx
    heifer, **8**
    milch, xxxiii, xxxviii
    red, **61, 72**
    stropper, xxxiii
    white, **72**
    wintering, **31**